NORTH ATLANTIC ODYSSEY

Sailing to the Arctic Circle

To Dominic and Eleanor:
   This book is dedicated to you.
It is a summons to gather up the
courage to go and live your
dreams.

10/12/89

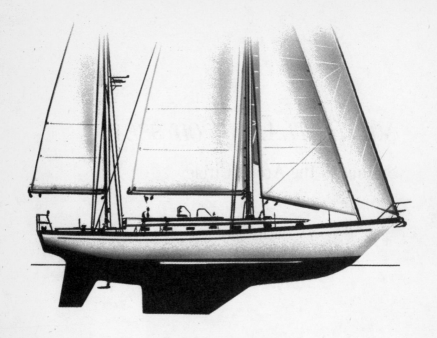

FREE SPIRIT

Specifications

Length overall 47'
Length on waterline 37'
Beam 13'10"
Draft 6'0"
Displacement 32,000 pounds
Ballast 12,000 pounds
Designer: Ted Brewer
Type of vessel: Mariner 47
Builder: Mariner Yacht Co.
        Rochester, N.H.

NORTH ATLANTIC ODYSSEY

Sailing to the Arctic Circle

Robert S. Gould

St. Martin's Press

New York

Also by Robert S. Gould:

The Boater's Medical Companion (Cornell Maritime Press)

Design by Susan Hood

Library of Congress Cataloging-in-Publication Data

Gould, Robert S.
    North Atlantic odyssey : sailing to the Arctic Circle / Robert S.
  Gould.
      p. cm.
    ISBN 0-312-02956-X
    1. Sailing—North Atlantic Ocean.   2. Sailing—North Sea.
  I. Title.
  GV817.N73G68   1989
  797.1'24'091631—dc19   89-30152
                                                              CIP

First Edition
10 9 8 7 6 5 4 3 2 1

*T*his book is dedicated to the many wonderful, warm people who so graciously received us in Ireland, Norway, England, and France, and the many helpful souls who openly assisted us in dozens of other ports around the Atlantic.

To my marvelous family: my wife, Cindy, and our children, Peter, Elizabeth, and John, this work is a testament to the value of struggle and common purpose. My love to you all.

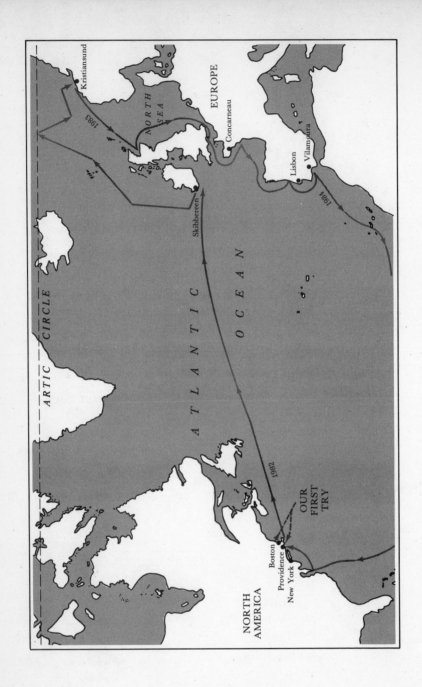

Contents

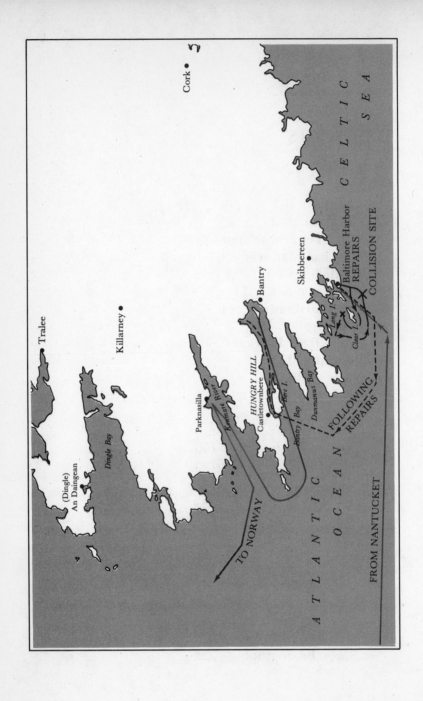

Preface

*T*his book is a celebration of life. It is the story of a dreamer who lived his dream, of a family that learned to pull together, and of people on both sides of the Atlantic who recognized and appreciated the chance to become a part of the romance and heroism of that dream.

This book describes a world where the opportunity to seek adventure still exists. It is a story of heart-warming hospitality, where strangers become friends and strange lands become a second home. This is a tale in which man meets his destiny with courage and conviction. It is meant to send a message to all: Never give up one's dreams.

Above all, this is a story of the sea: the majesty and power of the great ocean that tempts us and taunts us, leaves us speechless with ecstasy, weakened from her fury, and enriched by her endless beauty. To all who would venture upon her, explore her inner secrets, bathe in her soothing silkiness, paint her moods, or linger in her harbors, this narrative is intended for you.

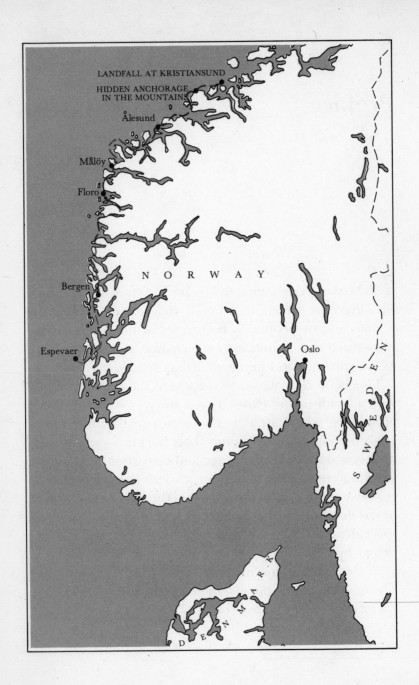

CHAPTER 1

False Start

*T*he day dawned dark and dreary. Rain clouds raced over a sea of gray and a cold, damp wind blew down the channel, giving a wintry chill to the early June day. The decorative flags by the nearby office buildings danced to the rhythms of the east wind and chattered to each other, each on its own pole. Gulls swooped and dipped, curtsying to the elements. One in particular, despite straining wings, hung almost motionless as she drove against the tempest. Then she banked and disappeared over the arching bridge that marked the end of the harbor, a bridge festooned with blinking red and green lights. Underneath, the darkened water bubbled past rotten old wharves and decayed pilings to the locks leading into Boston's Charles River.

At midday, *Free Spirit* tugged uneasily at her lines as if she were anxious about leaving her berth and somewhat uneasy about the long voyage ahead. A small knot of people gathered around the heavily loaded white yacht. A strong gust of wind laced with tiny rain droplets added a mournful note to the unreality of the scene. The skipper of the vessel, that's me, distracted, grubby, and tired, attempted to put on a brave face for the benefit of the friends and relatives assembled for the farewell party. But it was a thinly disguised front for anxiety and fatigue and it fooled no one. We were celebrating in preparation for our departure, yet it was not to be. At 11:00 P.M. the night before our planned departure, the kerosene furnace had blown up with a puff of smoke, and flames poured out the chimney. A cloud of choking, acrid soot billowed through the boat and three youngsters aching for sleep were sent out onto the dock. The oldest, a young man just reaching the first stage on his climb toward maturity, would find many challenges in the months ahead. The youngest, at the age of ten today tried to show how much he knew about the boat to the school friends who'd come to see him off. Our daughter, excited about the adventure but devastated to be leaving friends at home, would soon discover unique capabilities she'd never known she had. Finally, my wife and companion of twenty years, barely five feet tall and weary from helping me battle the heater into the wee hours of the morning, hustled here and there, trying to be a good hostess for the crowd of well-wishers.

We had recruited a second man, forty years old, from an earlier Bermuda trip. He had proved to be a valuable crew member in the past. Strong, resilient, and with a good sense of humor and a hardy sense of duty, Wayne was to be the linchpin holding the rest of the crew together. He and I would share many of the heavier and more difficult tasks. He was to be my alter ego. Who could imagine the fate that was to befall this veteran sailor?

Another gust of wind, and now the rain began to fall in earnest. Reports from those who had passed the sea wall in Swampscott on their way to the harbor indicated that huge seas were breaking over the wall. Quietly, telling no one, I made the decision not to leave that day. The farewell party could go on, but the broken heater and the bad weather—one does not challenge the North Atlantic unless all signs are favorable.

For two weeks now, the customary westerly winds had been absent, and instead strong easterlies blew from the sea. Marching across New England, a series of low-pressure systems had drenched the area and caused the most serious floods in decades. Storm and tornado watches flashed across the country. The sun seemed to have fled permanently to a nether land that had swallowed up its precious life-giving warmth. The day was cold, like so many during the previous week, and the temperature was about forty-two degrees. It seemed that winter had never released her icy grip, yet it was the eighth of June, the day chosen for our departure, the day planned in such detail so many months ago.

Elizabeth, our middle child, age sixteen (by ten days), had read her horoscope and learned that she would be leaving on a long voyage on June tenth. I shrugged. I had the modern intellectual's disdain for things unscientific. I didn't believe in astrology or horoscopes, but it was weird, this weather and the delay it was obviously going to cause. This was just the first of a number of unplanned events that were to alter the course of our adventure. Who in modern-day America would believe that life could be so beyond one's control? That damn heater! Everything on the boat had been checked and rechecked to make sure it was in proper working order. The heater had worked all spring. Why had it broken now?

Gradually, the well-wishers drifted away. Grandparents, torn by the fear of possible calamity, stayed longer and still asked whether we might change our minds about going.

The champagne bottles were cleaned up and the crew were left to consider our problems. I got on the phone to Connecticut and spoke with the distributor for the heater. The response was discouraging: There was no place in Boston to get it repaired; no serviceman could come; if I wanted the heater fixed, I should bring it to Connecticut. Being an extremely stubborn man, I rejected this solution as impractical and took the thing apart again, determined not to be defeated.

This kerosene furnace, made in Sweden, had been sold to me in lieu of the diesel furnace specified in the original contract because it was "cleaner and better." In actuality, the boat manufacturer had saved $2,000 by installing this type, but I didn't discover this until I attended a boat show after I had purchased the boat. A new diesel furnace would have cost the manufacturer $3,000. The kerosene heater had cost him about $1,000. The difference went to his bottom-line profit. I would eventually deliver that heater to the bottom of the ocean.

Covered with soot, knuckles torn from working in the cramped cubby where the heater had been stuffed, I fired up the furnace again. This time it worked! The elation of success lasted for fifteen minutes, and then the thing exploded in flames and I hurried to shut it down again.

Huddled that night in my sleeping bag, I could not sleep. Should I chance the North Atlantic and its attendant cold and wet without a heater? *Damn!* A delay at this point would throw off the precise clockwork of the entire trip. Wayne had only four weeks of vacation, and it would take three to make the crossing. The heater would have to be repaired in Connecticut. This was the first of many lessons I was to learn: Never plan a sailing adventure so tightly that you don't have room for changes. Unplanned contingencies or bad weather can alter those plans.

Getting up at four in the morning, I took the entire contraption out of the boat. It was disassembled by five-thirty, and I was in a taxi by six-fifteen heading for the airport with the heater tucked into a large box on the seat beside me. The shop was a small, second-floor office with a large back room devoted to repairs. It was a one-man show. The guy was salesman, United States representative, and the only expert on repairs in the country. He was very helpful and had it fixed within a couple of hours. I had difficulty following his explanation of what went wrong, and instead I concentrated on his instructions on how to reinstall the unit. By three in the afternoon I was back, $350 poorer, but elated. The thing was fixed and I had it reinstalled by six o'clock.

The folks at Constitution Marina in the Charlestown section of Boston were super. Randy, the marina's general handyman and watchman, a naturally ebullient and friendly fellow, six feet, three inches tall, made us some bolts for the heater. One enthusiastic friend of his had the map of Ireland in his features. He bubbled over with fervor about our pending voyage. On our summer-long trip across the Atlantic to Norway, Ireland would be the first landfall. Before we left, he solemnly placed a sticker of a four-leafed clover on our cabin top. Cindy and the kids guarded this emblem religiously, and indeed we all felt that it would somehow watch over us on the crossing. Everyone at the marina, including secretaries Pat and Cheryl, and Bob, the owner, went out of their way to be helpful. At a party thrown for us a fellow named Chuck, owner of a little Freedom catboat, told us he thought of us as heroes. What an absurd idea! I was simply a middle-aged, middle-class workaholic who'd suddenly been faced with the realization that if I was ever going to do something adventurous, I had better do it now.

My family made their decisions independently—each of them with some misgivings. Peter, seventeen, and Elizabeth, then fifteen, decided to come along almost from the day I had announced the trip the previous December. Peter had been disappointed that he could not join me two years earlier on a sail to Bermuda. The thought of an ocean sail stirred his sense of adventure. With his dark brown eyes and curly, dark brown hair, he presented quite a contrast to his sandy blond sister and to his light blond little brother, John. Despite being almost eighteen he had not yet gained his full growth and did not do so for another two years. Only five feet, six inches tall and weighing 125 pounds, he was well proportioned and coordinated, and quite athletic. He got along well in school and had several close friends. The fact that he was shorter than most of his peers never seemed to faze him, and they treated him as an equal. (A few years later he shot up like a sapling.) Somehow, this equanimity with friends and peers never translated into an easy relationship with his younger sister. Growing up, they seemed to fight a perpetual battle that had only recently begun to show signs of truce. For the first time, Peter respected his sister's taste in clothes, would ask her advice about peer issues, and generally listened to her opinions. He was on the wrestling team at school and was an extremely talented student who ranked high in his class. Math was his forte, yet he had never displayed much interest in the algebraic problems connected with piloting a small vessel. "I was comfortable with and confident in the boat, but not in my own abilities," Peter later confessed.

"Dad had always done it all. Somehow, though, I thought that I could learn, and that I was strong enough to do anything." None of the family had delved into the art of sailing as I had. All seemed content to come along and let me take care of the details.

Elizabeth, since the age of two, had always insisted on doing everything that her older brother did. Her immediate enthusiasm for the trip was perhaps a knee-jerk response to Peter's. If he was going, she was damned if she would be left behind. Always bright and alert, she gave off an aura of self-control and confidence that she did not always feel. About five feet, three inches tall, with long, straight hair and serious brown eyes, she was a pretty figure whenever she showed her friends around the boat. She was quick to smile or laugh, her eyes flashing warmth and her even white teeth setting off a flawless complexion. When asked six years later to comment on herself, she said, "I was innocent, naive, and flirtatious. I learned just how big the world was and, therefore, that there were endless social opportunities available to me."

John, at ten, was less involved in the rivalry that occupied his older siblings. He had bright blue eyes that laughed and straight, blond hair, and he adored playing sports. Two broken legs in the previous two years—the result of playground accidents—had, however, put him on the sidelines. He had originally planned to fly over with his mother and meet us in Ireland, but gradually he became seduced by the romance of the adventure and signed aboard. He was a sweet, cautious, outgoing child. He wasn't shy, and made friends wherever he went. "I was very afraid of sailing across the Atlantic, but I didn't want to show it because Peter and Elizabeth didn't. Ever since *Little Dove* [an earlier twenty-three-foot pocket cruiser we had owned] I have had the fear of being out of control in big waves. I was afraid that something would go wrong and there'd be no one around to help. I was afraid that something would happen to Dad and we would all be lost. In spite of this, I was the only one of us kids who loved boats. Ever since I was a kid I've rowed and used the outboard motor, and enjoyed being around the water."

That left my wife Cindy with a major dilemma. Her whole family was going to hell in a cork bottle. What would she do with her life if they all just disappeared? In April, she took the plunge. As she put it, "I decided, finally, that we'd either make it together or we wouldn't, but we should not be separated. Although I thought that Bob had gone mad the first time he mused aloud about the exciting possibility of the family sailing together across the Atlantic, never did I dream, at the time, that it would become a reality. I asked for and received a leave of absence from my job at Xerox, so I could then concentrate on the terrors of the passage." Cindy was excited and eager, yet fearful of the possibilities. Nearly every night after her decision had been made, she'd wake up in a cold sweat with another "what if" question for me. "What if you have a heart attack?" "What if we get run down?" At least when I had sailed to Bermuda, she was able to fly there and meet me and have a wonderful week in the sun. I suppose for some people that's really the ideal way to go cruising. Let some other sucker deliver the boat. You just fly there and enjoy it.

Cindy is a plucky gal. Although filled with concerns and worries, she hangs in there with the best of them when the chips are down. I had met her years earlier at a party in Lewiston, Maine. I was a freshman at Bates and she a sophomore in high school. We sat at a piano and played duets together. Five years later our paths crossed again. I called her for a date and within two weeks had proposed. She was barely five feet tall, vivacious, weighed ninety-five pounds, and was the leader of Connecticut College's singing group, the Schwiffs. We fell head over heels for each other. She quickly discovered that I had an unorthodox and adventurous soul. Accustomed to eating hot dogs and little else, she'd been appalled when, on our first date, I ordered frog's legs for dinner. From then on, I led her from one adventure to another. On our honeymoon, we drove across the country in our VW with only a general idea of our itinerary. We camped out and stayed in cheap motels, averaging five dollars per night. After one week, we met another young couple who had managed to stay together three whole months. We were amazed. How had they stayed together so long? We had already had three petty fights that seemed awfully tough back then. Looking back as I write this now, with twenty-six years of marriage behind us, it seems pretty funny.

The previous summer's family cruise to Nova Scotia had given everyone a short experience of a couple of days at sea. Ideal weather made it perfect. I kept telling Cindy that once she made the Atlantic crossing everything else would seem easy. Otherwise, every time we had to cross from Ireland to Norway or make any other open water passage, it would be a major trauma for her. Indeed, so it would prove, but little did I realize at that moment what it would be like for any of us.

The next morning the sun shone. The wind had swung around to the south and all portents indicated favorable conditions for beginning our adventure. Our large, white yacht, forty-seven feet on deck and so much more stately than her harbor- and coastbound sisters, seemed quite diminutive against the background of oceangoing vessels lashed to the enormous bollards of the city's commercial docks. The gathering in of fenders and lines, the movement away from the pier lent a feeling of relief to all aboard. The SatNav had been programmed the night before, its waypoints showing just under a thousand miles to our first turning point. The day was beautiful and the big yacht heeled over gently in the breeze. Ironically, Elizabeth's horoscope had been right. We were leaving on June tenth.

Ten miles out of Boston, our Hood Stoway roller-furling gear jammed, and since we were within striking distance, we hove into Marblehead for some professional assistance. In order to handle the enormous sails of a big yacht like *Free Spirit*, we had chosen to have the mainsail on roller-furling. It could, therefore, roll up like a window shade into the mast. Leading to the cockpit were a series of lines to haul the sail out or roll it back up. The forward sail or genoa was also on roller-furling so it could be doused from the cockpit with less risk than if we had to go forward on deck to drop a flogging half-acre of sail in heaving seas and howling winds. This forward or headsail is sometimes called a yankee, because the sail's lower edge is high enough so one can see beneath the sail.

In racing boats, genoas are often deck sweepers; that is to say that they come down to the deck. These are powerful sails for light breezes but are impractical on an ocean-cruising yacht. I preferred to see where we were going rather than sail with the extra half-knot of additional speed.

It was to be the last time we would be able to count on boatyard help for over a year! The problem was a jammed sheet-stopper. Furling system lines at the mast led through a series of blocks to a Hood line driver winch on the coach roof. These lines passed through a sheet-stopper engineered to allow one to jam the lines so they would not move. This was an unnecessary complication and was corrected by simply eliminating the stopper. We finally set off again at 2:30 P.M. the same day.

An unreality permeated our first hours at sea, and this was heightened for me by mental exhaustion. Loss of sleep due to the heater fire put us all on edge. Peter had just completed final exams and college boards. With these behind him, he looked forward to the challenges of a transatlantic voyage but was somewhat troubled by the lack of definition of his role in the crew. Neither child nor adult, his memories were of a time as a child when he had limited responsibilities for ship's duties on short coastal cruises. He had missed the trip to Bermuda two years earlier because of a fractured hand. The following year, he had been a very valuable assistant during *Free Spirit*'s maiden voyage to Nova Scotia. He was able to take a trick at the helm, as could the other children, and he was also helpful in handling the big sails that a forty-seven-foot boat carried. Whenever it was necessary to do heavy work, he was always at my side to give me a hand. He and his sister had steered *Free Spirit* with an emergency tiller for hours at a time on the return trip from Nova Scotia. However, the length of that trip was brief and the drama of losing our steering in a gale at midnight only served to accentuate the potential dangers of the ocean. As we now departed on a far more challenging voyage, I sensed that prior experiences we had all shared made each one of us somber and reflective, as if we suddenly recognized the serious potential for major problems in this supreme adventure.

Elizabeth had also just finished her exams. She took them seriously and I could tell she was relieved that they were over. She was obviously glad to be out of school, but some numbness and sadness could be detected in her usually bubbling demeanor. Although she had signed up for the voyage early on, she had had second thoughts the past few months, and at this point was an unwilling participant. She hated leaving all her friends and did not look forward to the discomforts of the sea. On several occasions she had begged me to allow her to stay home for the summer. I simply would not countenance such a thing. The thought of leaving my sixteen-year-old daughter for a summer without some supervision was simply appalling. Moreover, our object was to have a family adventure, with everyone participating and sharing in the interdependence required for survival. If ever an experience could enhance a family's growth and togetherness, this one was it. Without actually mandating that she come (she later said I was firmer than that!), I somehow convinced her of this.

Wayne, feeling the strain of responsibility as the only truly experienced backup to the skipper, was jovial and outwardly relaxed as the ship leaped over the sparkling seas. Wayne was powerfully built, forty years old, a sergeant in the Needham police force. With his high forehead, sharply chiseled bulldog features, and steady, gray eyes, he looked like the quintessential cop. He also was a sailing nut. He and his wife, Holly, owned a thirty-six-foot sloop and they sailed it winter and summer out of Newport, Rhode Island. Wayne had sailed to Bermuda with me two years earlier and had proved a valuable crew. Always willing to lend a hand, he was strong and capable of handling any task. I felt comfortable having him along as my alter ego. Wayne is an extremely intelligent and philosophical man. We had spent several evenings in years past talking of human nature, international communism, and issues such as the arms race. "I loved Wayne," Elizabeth said, "because he always treated me as if I were someone special. He would call me 'princess' and mean it. He was also very good-looking." Peter liked Wayne too, "He was the kind of guy you could trust." Cindy couldn't think of anyone who would better be able to share a small space with our family than Wayne. He was a great guy, well centered.

The sun was shining for the first time in two weeks as we headed east. Although the skies were clear and pleasant and the wind was from the south, the previous two weeks of stormy weather, high winds, and monsoonlike rains suggested that there would be more to come.

As the afternoon wore on, the winds lightened and shifted around to the northeast. There was still a lumpy sea from the east with eight- to nine-foot waves. We motorsailed into it. The leftover slop from the previous two weeks gave *Free Spirit* a lively action, and seasickness began to infiltrate the crew. First young John, then Cindy, and finally Elizabeth hit the rail. I felt queasy, and Peter and Wayne were very silent. We powered that night and into the next day. By noon the wind was up but from the northeast. We cut the engine and held a course of 120°. This was more southeast than I preferred, but in this stuff the boat sailed far better than she motored.

Lunch was a pick-me-up affair. No one wanted to do any work. By our second night at sea everyone was still seasick despite the use of Transderm (scopolamine patches) that we had placed behind our ears. With the wind still from the northeast and the crew unable to keep watches, I decided to heave to for the night.

When successfully accomplished, heaving to can be used

to lessen the pounding that a ship must take in heavy weather, easing the strain on both gear and crew. It is an accomplishment to take a plunging, tossing sailing vessel and, with a thrust of the wheel, turn her into a peaceful filly, grazing on the pasture of the open sea amid the fury of a storm. Traditionally, heaving to involves shortening sail and changing tacks without changing the lead for the headsail. The mainsail and jib are both strapped in tightly by hauling in on their sheets. This flattens both sails and will make them less likely to flap. The boat is then sailed up into the wind and through the eye of the wind to come about on the opposite tack. The jib sheet is not released as it usually would be. The small jib is caught aback with its clew held to windward. The wheel is then turned back in the other direction as if to sail back onto the opposite tack. With a backed jib, the boat will not develop enough power to make that tack and will simply stop, back down, and try again. If you lash the wheel or tiller in this position, she should continue to stay there.

The effort was a complete failure. This was the first time I had tried to get *Free Spirit* to heave to under such conditions and she refused to do so. With a backed storm staysail and reefed main, her wheel hard over to bring the head into the wind, she would gradually fall off until she was beam on to the seas. This led to an extremely uncomfortable motion as she rolled heavily in the ten-foot seas. I sat out with her in the stormy night and studied the situation. I had to find a way to ease the motion aboard or I'd have no crew left.

It was apparent to me that the bow was being blown off. The reefed mainsail could not hold her up to the wind. What if I dropped the storm staysail? Working my way forward with my harness clipped to the jacklines, I dropped the flogging canvas as large, dark crests loomed to windward and slipped out beneath our bow. With the storm staysail secured, I returned to the cockpit and again threw the wheel over into the wind. Her reefed mainsail, trimmed amid ships, was able to drive us up into the wind but did not have enough power to drive her through the eye onto the opposite tack. She headed up into the wind and sat there like a snowy white sea bird, dipping and curtsying to the seas with a ladylike motion.

The gentleness won me over and I slipped below to get some sleep. All was quiet. Everyone was in their own cocoon of misery. I crawled in next to young John and cuddled him in my arms. How could I have even dreamed of subjecting this wonderful family of mine to such brutal agony? I dozed off without an answer.

From Cindy's perspective: "Heaving to was torture. It had been our plan to keep five in berths at night with a sixth person on watch." With the forward vee berth virtually uninhabitable because of the motion, we were down to five berths. Since I was in the double berth with John, Cindy, being small, decided that she would double up with Peter in his capacious single berth. Unfortunately, he was on the down side and could rest against his lee cloth. She, however, had to hang onto the mattress until she fell asleep. Once she relaxed, her grip would loosen, and she'd fall into Peter with a solid thwack. Peter would utter a moan or groan and cry out, "Mom!" With a mumbled "Sorry," Cindy would climb back up, only to have the whole process repeat itself again and again throughout the night.

Our third day at sea dawned dismal and cold. The wind was still out of the east. I got up at 2:30 A.M. to start sailing and got clobbered with a boarding sea that soaked me through my open foul-weather jacket. I stumbled back down below to change four layers of clothes and crawled back into my bunk. At dawn I arose to find that we had no power in the two big 120-amp Surette batteries that controlled all systems on board. Since we had no autopilot, Wayne took the wheel. Our separate engine battery, which had its own alternator, continued to operate, allowing us to start the engine. However, no power flowed to the dead house batteries. I took apart the wiring harness leading to the alternators and found a wire that was shorting out on the casing because of damaged insulation. Some electrical tape and a general cleaning of all connectors and we were back in business. The alternator sent a charge to the batteries and within several hours, they were functioning normally.

Although I have had lots of experience in handling boats, this trip was my first exposure to the need for innumerable repairs. I was ill prepared for this. Nowhere in my background had I been required to solve mechanical or electrical problems. My only saving grace was a fierce determination to figure everything out myself and solve any problem that arose. I had planned carefully for such mechanical failures, of course. I had copies of all the manuals to every piece of equipment aboard, and I had made an effort to read through the manuals before setting out to sea. Whenever I didn't understand something important, I called the company and asked them what they meant. The shorted wire was the first of many, many repairs we had to make at sea or in out-of-the-way ports. We quickly learned that when you are hundreds of miles from civilization, you must become totally self-reliant. You must trust in your ability to figure out anything and everything. Safety and survival depend on it.

Cindy relays her thoughts: "I learned about my family

at sea. Peter and Elizabeth wasted no energy worrying about things that might happen, while I always anticipated problems, whether they were likely to occur or not. When I raised concerns, I noticed that their reaction was more like their father's: 'When that happens, Mom, we'll figure out a way to deal with it.' John, on the other hand, at the more vulnerable age of ten, would ask questions in a tone that I could relate to. I could hear his worry and fear as he watched his father working to repair the refrigeration system. 'Daddy, what if you can't fix it? Will all the food spoil?' Bob, on the other hand, had had twenty years of practice as a surgeon to learn how to face challenging, difficult, life-and-death problems. This experience, coupled with his stubborn refusal ever to give up, enabled us to weather a number of harrowing and even life-threatening situations. Somehow, no matter how difficult the problem, he faced it with what seemed to me to be almost a joy at a new challenge."

Ocean Passages for the World is a book published by the British Admiralty office describing the various routes recommended for sailing ships. The basic principle is that sailing ships prefer to sail with rather than against the wind. To cross the Atlantic, taking a northern route from New England to Ireland virtually guarantees having the wind and currents at your back. That, at least, is the wisdom of the written word. It ignores, however, the effect of low-pressure systems and the easterlies that they bring in. Downwind in the westerlies to Europe. Ha! What nonsense!

Oranges were the only nourishment that the crew could take. Poor little John had been wrung out on the rail over and over and had finally succumbed to exhaustion and sleep. Gradually he was able to take orange slices and occasional pieces of toast and finally, after the fourth day, he seemed to be all right. Cindy, all ninety-five pounds of her, threatened to vanish entirely if she didn't begin to take nourishment. She, likewise, had an uplifting of soul and body on the fourth day and seemed to be regaining her indomitable spirit. We hoped to celebrate our twentieth anniversary at sea, crossing the Atlantic. "I never felt my normal, energetic self at sea. That was the one disappointing thing for me. I thought that after a few days I would get my sea legs, but it never happened during the crossing."

Elizabeth, forced into her bunk by continued mal de mer, had at least been able to read four books in as many days. She was now able to take watches along with me and her older brother. Peter, although tired by the boat motion, had largely remained unaffected by the pitching except for an increasing lethargy. I found it slightly amusing to watch from my seat at the chart table as he slowly rose up from his bunk to get his mother a sweatshirt. It seemed to take him forever to make the decision to get the shirt and then actually accomplish the task. We all found it amazingly difficult to perform any task those first days at sea. It had taken Cindy four hours to ask for the sweatshirt and another eight before she could get up to put it on. She just clung to it in her berth, shivering with cold, yet could not summon the energy to rise to a sitting position.

As we progressed to the far side of Georges Bank and passed through out umpteenth fishing fleet, all of us except Wayne were beginning to get our sea legs and stand our watches. Poor Wayne, staunch friend and helper, never one to complain, gradually became weaker. He couldn't even take the orange slices I offered him. He attempted to make light of the situation and held a small can of tomato juice that I had handed him. After studying the can seriously for a moment, he handed it back and said haughtily, "It says on the label that it's supposed to be served chilled!" We laughed, but I continued to watch him closely, for by then he had taken nothing for two days. Up to this point, I had tried all the old remedies I was familiar with. We had started with Transderm patches; when Wayne began to get sick, I gave him Compazine by injection; we even tried acupressure. Nothing helped. I spoke to him seriously about the importance of taking at least some fluids. He looked at me gravely and told me that he couldn't even *imagine* putting anything into his mouth. At that point, I decided to pull out the intravenous fluids that I had carefully stuffed into the bilge for just this eventuality. Although I am a physician by profession, I had hoped not to run a hospital ship, but duty called. On the fifth day, despite four liters of intravenous fluids, Wayne still could not take anything by mouth. Stabilized but weak as a kitten, he asked to go back. The decision was really hard for him and we were all depressed, but his health and safety were foremost in our minds.

We therefore turned, recrossed the wide Georges Bank, and made our way toward Nantucket. The days of pounding beats gradually dimmed behind the tears of frustration and failure. *Free Spirit*, with the wind behind her, tore through the water like a young thoroughbred headed back to her stable. We arrived at the harbor two days later at midnight. With no lighted markers to outline the tricky harbor entrance, we ran aground on the way in. Another lesson learned. Never try to make an unfamiliar harbor at night without absolutely clear markers. My exhaustion clouded my judgment and didn't allow for the alternative of anchoring in the open roadstead off the island. The sea is a firm teacher and she presses her points home without mercy.

We rowed an anchor out toward where we thought the channel was and tried to kedge off, but were unable to move her. It was a dark, moonless night and a light fog hung over the waters. Eventually, at 2:30 A.M., I was able to raise a commercial tow that hauled us off the mud, and we followed them shamefacedly into the harbor. Finally at a berth, we collapsed and slept. Wayne's seasickness cleared as soon as we tied up. He felt terrible about being responsible for ending our trip, but what choice did he or any of us have? The next day I called Al, a friend who was to have joined us in Ireland, and asked him to take Wayne's place. He needed some time to see if he could sort out business responsibilities, but would try to join us in Nantucket in a few days.

At this point, thoroughly exhausted, with all my resources seemingly gone, with willing but inexperienced and not truly enthusiastic children, and with a wife who had lacked any fervor for my crazy project in the first place, I was ready to quit the venture and simply spend a pleasant summer cruising in Maine. It was Cindy who insisted on going! Unbelievable! She reminded me how much work and planning had gone into the venture and how much I had hoped to cruise in Europe. She was willing to try again if I was. What an amazing woman! This was the same woman who, fourteen years earlier, had thought I was crazy when I pulled into the yard with a twelve-foot sailboard before we had any living room furniture, lamps, or shrubbery for our new house. Sailing to Bermuda had been a mad adventure, but I had made it—in spite of four major storms. This gave her some confidence in my abilities. Prior to that she had never been willing to go with me out of sight of land, and now she was urging me to persevere in this seemingly impossible quest. Peter described his feelings: "I was terribly disappointed when the decision was made to turn back. I was even more horrified that we might go to Maine instead. When we finally decided to give it another try, I was elated."

Nantucket was great fun for the kids and just the right place to lick our wounds. A local pharmacist was a great help to me in replacing our depleted medical supplies and he and his wife were tremendously supportive and encouraging.

The Nantucket interlude gave me time to reflect on everything that had brought us here, to the brink of our great adventure.

CHAPTER 2

The Dawn

*A*fter fourteen years of medical practice, I needed a sabbatical. Two weeks of vacation simply would no longer do. "Let's take a year off and sail to Europe." "You've got to be kidding. We can't afford to do that!" That short exchange between Cindy and me was how it all started. As it turned out, she was right. We couldn't afford it. Neither could we afford not to. We were both in our early forties, each embroiled in interesting careers, our older children well along in high school. But life moves on, and unless one continues to move along and grow with it, one runs the risk of being left behind—of suddenly realizing that one is too old to do all the things that seemed so enticing. For years I have dreamed of sailing to far seas, of exploring distant places—Europe, the south seas, the Orient. Well, now I know it's all possible. We've come this far and we can do it all.

It all grew slowly. In 1968, I completed my residency in urology at the Lahey Clinic in Boston. Internship in surgery at the New England Medical Center had involved 132 hours a week on call at the hospital, and walking a new baby 2 to 3 hours a night during my scant time at home. (Peter never slept after midnight for the first two years of his life.) This essential training in the ability to function without sleep was very important: It helped me to become a skipper who could easily awaken at night and be immediately capable of handling crises at sea.

Nineteen sixty-eight was a dramatic year for me. I opened my new practice and bought my first sailboat—a twelve-foot sailing skiff. I simply drove home with it one Saturday afternoon. It had cost me, complete with trailer, the grossly exorbitant sum of $450, new! Cindy was horrified. How could I dream of spending such a fortune without consulting her? Little did either of us dream that this was but a pauper's beginning in the ever expanding, ever more extravagant world of yacht financing. I paid for my first boat by check. My most recent one was financed by overextending myself to the extreme.

Dreams, dreams, dreams—focusing more and more on sailing as a way of communing with nature and with the essential me. Dreams of voyages, dreams of freedom, perhaps all stemming from the constrictions and responsibilities of a twenty-four-hour-a-day, seven-day-a-week solo medical practice. I devoured books, hundreds upon hundreds of them, in my fanatic devotion to the dream and an attempt to ease the ache of desire, a desire for excitement, adventure, and exploration. I cleaned out the Wellesley Free Library—ten books a week. I began buying books and now have two ceiling-high bookcases filled with books on sailing: the instructional books, the guide books, and, most importantly, the cruising experiences: *Dove, Two against Cape Horn, On the Wind's Way, The Romantic Challenge*, Robinson, Stuemer, Street, and Hiscock—names became personalities as real to me as life itself. I especially recommend to the novice sailor Richard Henderson's *The Cruiser's Compendium*, Donald Street's *The Ocean-Sailing Yacht*, and K. Adlard Coles's *Heavy-Weather Sailing*. For pure enjoyment read William Snaith's *On the Wind's Way*, or any of Tristan Jones's works or those of Lin and Larry Pardey. To savor the ocean as it really can be, read *Through the Roaring Forties*, written by Vito Dumas, or Bernard Moitessier's *Joshua*. Live the ocean with Sir Francis Chichester in *The Romantic Challenge* or Dame Naomi James in *Alone around the World*. *Dove* by Robin Lee Graham, *Southwest in Wanderer II* by Susan and Eric Hiscock, and Joe Richard's *Princess* also make for excellent reading. To help you with navigation, I recommend Hewitt Schlereth's *Commonsense Celestial Navigation*, the only book on the subject I have ever been able to understand. Medical subjects for the long-distance voyager are covered in Peter Eastman's *Advanced First Aid Afloat* and my own thoughts on the subject are covered in *The Boater's Medical Companion*, published by Cornell Maritime Press. Finally, to plan ocean crossings *Ocean Passages for the World*, published by the Hydrographer of the Navy, British Admiralty Office, is extremely helpful.

I was involved; I lived them all; and I moved up to a twenty-three-footer, a Paceship, built in Mahone Bay, Nova Scotia. It was a strong, tough, real little sea boat. I named her *Little Dove*; after all she was but a foot shorter than Robin Lee Graham's round-the-worlder. That first summer with her, I simply took off. I took nine weeks off, to be exact. Friends at the hospital told me that I would lose my practice and have to start all over. It didn't happen. When I returned after Labor Day, I was as busy as ever.

I sailed. My God, how I sailed. I went out every single

day but two of those blessed nine weeks. I went out in rain, in fog, in sunshine, and in storm. I tried everything I had ever read—plotting a course, reefing, heaving to. I gloried in the experience. Buzzards Bay became the proving ground for all my dreams, and loomed larger than fantasy, my nirvana with *Little Dove* my winged steed. Those weeks were pure glory, tinged with the golden aura of peace and freedom.

Not all of our experiences were, of course, as free from problems. Disasters seemed geared either to fine-tune our skills or tear our hopes asunder. The metamorphosis from a landlubber to a sailor is, after all, a painstaking process. It is not a neat, natural evolution like the creation of a butterfly. It is the result of a series of mistakes that the would-be sailor must abide in order to qualify as a seasoned seaman. This process must be endured. No amount of planning or intelligence or reading can substitute for the actual ordeal of disaster at sea. The following experience is but one of many that helped forge the development of this sailor.

On an early summer day in 1974, I arose at dawn to warm, flowing breezes coming across the bay. The previous week had been miserable, rainy and cool. Thus, when this clear though blustery day broke out, I set off with light heart and extra canvas for the very special pleasure of pitting my little boat against the wily bay.

Little Dove responded beautifully to the initial tack from our mooring. The neat, weathered shingled houses with white trim, characteristic of Salters Point, glistened in the sunshine. As we drove out from the protective lee of the sweeping shore, I felt the wind strength increase dramatically. I had the large #1 genoa set. She was a new sail and I wanted to see how *Little Dove* would handle under her glistening Dacron gown. With her gleaming decks and sparkling new sails, she brought a welling of pride leaping from my chest, and the slight glint of spray on my cheeks might as well have been tears of joy.

The wind was blowing about twenty-five knots with higher gusts. Four- to five-foot seas came rolling down the bay with intermittently breaking crests. I eased the main to spill some of the excess wind and suddenly spied the brigantine *Black Pearl* coming down the bay, rounding Mishaum Point and heading in toward Padanaram Harbor. We turned onto a beam reach to get a better look at this beautiful little ship. With the rail intermittently under water, I was forced to bear off in the gusts. In order to bring order out of the increasingly chaotic motion, I rolled a deep reef in the genny. My plan was to round Dumpling Rocks and set off on a broad reach with all sail drawing to try and catch my quarry before she reached the safety of the harbor.

Buccaneer visions passed before my eyes as I fantasized leading my crew of brave and stalwart lads on a boarding party of this armed and dangerous Spanish galleon. I was suddenly drawn with a snap back to reality. A sharp twang entered the periphery of my consciousness. I was appalled to see *Little Dove*'s mast arching forward like a palm tree in a hurricane. The genoa billowed out into a useless pillow. Something flew past my head with the snap of a bullwhip. I stared in the direction of the sound and there, heading directly for my forehead on the return swing, was the turnbuckle attached to the backstay. I ducked involuntarily and the backstay barely missed parting my head. It hung there for a moment and I reached for it to haul it in. In an instant, I found myself being lifted out of the cockpit. I quickly let go and landed on one knee on the floor. A decision had to be made quickly as to how to save the mast. I decided to head into the wind to try and place its pressure on the mast to push it up straight. This turned out to be exactly the wrong thing to do. As we headed into the wind, we headed into the seas, and with two or three pitches, *Little Dove* threw her mast into the ocean. It fell over the starboard bow, leaving my beautiful craft in a shambles. Wires and ropes and the foot of the mast were pushing and pounding at the deck and topsides of the hull. Off to our port side lay Dumpling Rocks, scarcely 500 yards away and downwind of our position. I scrambled out on deck, stumbling over the tangle of spars, sails, and wire, and dropped an anchor overboard. The mast slid overboard and began to pound against the side of the hull. I realized that I would have to cut it away to save the boat. I tethered the foot of the mast to the starboard stern cleat with a docking line and started to remove the clevis pins attaching the shrouds and head stay to the deck. With the boat tossing and pitching and with nothing to hold onto, it was incredibly difficult to move about the deck. Freed from tethers, the mast and sails floated safely to our stern. I hoped to tow them back to my mooring.

I started the little 6-hp outboard, weighed anchor, and proceeded with my tow. It soon became obvious that the large parachute of a sail was acting as a sea anchor and was affecting the steering. We drifted closer and closer to the rocks. The docking line parted under the strain and a stray line snagged the propeller of the outboard, leaving us without power or control. I rushed forward and again dropped anchor, now only fifty yards off the seething, surging surf. Exhausted and scared, I put in a call to Woods

Hole Coast Guard on my VHF transmitter. In my panic, I had forgotten that the antenna was now at the bottom of the bay.

With no response from the Coast Guard and nothing but static on the radio, it seemed prudent to try and unsnag the line around the propeller. In the pitching seas, this was a very wet project. Ten minutes spent half-submerged in the seaway and I had cut us free. We hauled anchor, motored away from the rocks, and limped into our mooring bereft of mast, boom, and sails. It was a discouraged and demoralized young sailor who stumbled up the hill to his seaside abode.

Far from being a totally wasted experience, this dismasting taught me several important lessons. First, I should never have trusted anyone else (a boatyard in this case) to secure the stays or shrouds to my boat. Second, it forced me to think about what I could have done differently to save the mast. With the backstay gone, I should first have hauled in on the mainsheet. This would have provided a stabilizing effect on the mast and acted as a substitute backstay. I then could have furled or dropped the genoa and then used the genoa halyard as a temporary backstay.

Harrowing as this episode was, it taught me a great deal. Without such exposure, the neophyte simply remains a boater. With each new challenge met, a seaman is formed who knows the pitfalls and how to avoid them.

I ordered a new mast and came back from work a month later to find that the yard hadn't even drawn the plans for the new spar. This, in spite of the fact that they had promised to have the new mast ready when I returned for the second half of my vacation. I then learned the art of gentle persuasion, and how effective it was simply to live at the boatyard and ask constantly what else I could do to help speed up the project. I was such a pain in the neck that they had me out of there in just two days—with my new mast.

Cindy wasn't quite as captivated by sailing as I was. She liked it when the sun shone and she loved a fresh breeze and exciting swells, but fog, cold, and rain were no fun for her and sailing in the dark scared her. For years thereafter, Cindy had a love-hate relationship with the boat and sailing. She loved day-sailing, but only if we didn't go too far. She liked to recognize familiar islands and didn't want to be too adventurous. She came down to meet me in Newport one summer several years ago to sail to Block Island. When we arrived, a summer fog put a dense shroud over the harbor. We waited for a day to see if it would clear. Upon learning that Block Island was ten miles off the coast and that I intended to get there, fog or no, she elected to stay ashore.

But nothing stays the same, and so it is with Cindy. Our children grew, she developed a stronger sense of self, and became involved with women's liberation. With an ever-growing sense of her own power, this tiny woman talked her way into a job with a computer company, learned programming, and finally became a top sales representative at Xerox. I was now married to a self-assured, self-reliant woman who could, if she chose, reasonably be a partner in my adventures.

Other sailing misadventures dotted our days on the water. Interspersed with the beautiful, serene days on the bay were dozens of accidents, groundings, and other problems that build a sailing experience that become the skipper's portfolio. There was the time we got caught in a snow and hail storm on April 29 in Hadley Harbor and tried to make it back to Mattapoisett. Leaky foul-weather gear laid me low that day. Cindy had to handle the tiller and take us into harbor. My hands were completely frozen and I finally collapsed with exhaustion and seasickness.

Not every day spent on the ocean is filled with drama or catastrophe—only the ones we tend to remember. Slipping my mooring at Salters Point one morning. I sailed down Buzzards Bay on an easy, rolling reach. My idea was to head to Newport, Rhode Island, one of many such trips. *Little Dove* had just been painted a beautifully rich, dark blue and she gleamed in the sun as her white sails hurried her along. She danced to a gentle and exotic beat as she glided down a pathway of shimmering light toward the hazy horizon. Cuttyhunk glowered at us as we slipped by, seeming to resent our passing her up for another beauty. She was a former love, however, and the excitement of sampling the glitter of Newport made her pale by comparison.

Although she was only twenty-two feet, nine inches long, my craft seemed as much an ocean-going vessel as any on the high seas. I lolled comfortably against a cushion propped up against the silent outboard motor, the tiller loosely tapping against the fingers of my right hand. The design alterations I had made the previous winter in the underwater configuration had changed a heavy bear of a tiller into a gentle little lamb. Mattapoisett Boatyard had tried to discourage me from fashioning a fiberglass skeg into her bottom and then changing the shape of the rudder to lead from the aft end of the skeg. This straight and true appendage would prove to point our way and hold our course whenever we were on the wind. The rudder was now used only to change direction.

Life was good. I would sail down to Newport and Cindy would meet me there in a few days. Evenings on the town and daytimes in the exotic shops would spice up the simple enjoyments of cruising. The sea slipped by and I nodded to old Cuttyhunk as she drifted astern. I hoped she would still welcome me in days to come. Navigation for me was by chart and compass. The only tools I had were a set of parallel rules, dividers, compass, and depth sounder. Buoy to buoy plotted in advance with time and distance were my security blanket. With Cuttyhunk long since settled below the horizon, and with the last buoy perhaps twenty minutes behind me, a heavy, moist fog dropped in for a visit. At first the sky remained quite bright, but as the haze thickened, it began to shut out the radiance of the day. I sat up and carefully scanned the waters as we drove along. The visibility was perhaps a hundred feet. I consulted the chart and, unfortunately, discovered I was in an area where buoys were few and far between.

I dug the ship's bell and horn out of their coffins and a mournful sonata began to ring from our cockpit. The melody sometimes was nearly lost in the swirling mist. At other times, it bounced back at us, almost as if the fog were laughing at us, enjoying its little joke. I sailed on, now wearing a warm jacket against the cool, damp air. One hour, perhaps two, passed and the hoped-for buoy never appeared. Gradually, I turned the bow north, to try and make landfall. I hoped that once I spotted land, we could follow the coast up to Narragansett Bay. Finally, I glimpsed some trees, boulders, a bit of beach. The depth sounder indicated that we were approaching shoal waters. *Little Dove* reached along the shore, just far enough offshore to safely clear all shallows. We drove on happily. No need for worry now. And then I saw them: barrels, hundreds of barrels, extending as far as I could see in front of us and out to sea. I drew close under sail and fell off as I saw the fish nets stretched between the wooden casks and leading to the beach. Grumbling to myself, I let myself lose the security of the shore; we headed to sea to try and round the outer perimeter of this man-made reef. For a full half hour we sailed into the bowels of the fog, beads of moisture clouding my eyes. And finally, they were gone. One minute they were there, dancing with malice at our discomfort, and suddenly, and without fanfare, there was nothing. I again turned southwest. Now I was truly lost. About the only thing I was sure of was that I was still north of New York.

Heading back toward shore well beyond the fish nets, I hoped again to spot the comforting coastline and follow it to its inevitability. Suddenly, with a heaving sigh almost like a hiss, a large boulder appeared on our port beam, easily within fifty feet of us. Almost at once, rocks began to appear on all sides. I fell onto the tiller, forcing the nimble little vessel to pirouette and head back to sea. We had narrowly missed bedding down for the night on Brenton Reef. Easing our way around the rocks, we found our way into Narragansett Bay. The fog was now, if anything, thicker. The visibility was down to about twenty feet. As we picked our way along the now obstruction-free shore, I began to hear horns and engines and bells as all sorts of vessels worked their way into and out of Newport Harbor. The cacophony was startling and disorienting. I remained totally on edge. Finally, I saw a number of sailboat masts and dropped anchor among the moored craft.

The fog lasted for days. Eventually I found the main

portion of the harbor and was able to give Cindy a call. The time spent waiting for the fog to lift allowed me to make some very personally satisfying sketches of some of the local mansions and lovely sailing craft at anchor. Yes, this was my first experience with Newport fog and no, it was not the last.

My navigation gradually improved, based on trial and error. I once sailed to Block Island on a beautiful summer day. Actually, *Little Dove* was so well balanced with her new skeg that she sailed herself there and I snoozed in the cockpit. When the island should be easily seen, I sat up and there it was. The only problem was that it looked round. I was totally disoriented. Which way was the harbor? I picked one direction, the wrong one of course, and by the time I realized my error I had to circumnavigate the entire island to find the entrance. This took an additional four hours.

One way to avoid this is to intentionally sail too far in one direction. Then when you must change your course the correct direction will be obvious. For example, if you are trying to find a harbor entrance in the fog, sail five or ten degrees to one side or the other (for instance ten degrees to the north of where you actually expect to find the harbor). Then when you near shore, turn south and you will find your entrance—if the harbor isn't exactly where you thought it was, at least you know that you will pass it. And that you're heading in the right direction.

Each experience taught its lessons, however, and over the years, mistakes came fewer and farther apart. After six years of sailing the New England coast, I was no longer making mistakes and I no longer missed harbors. Navigating in fog became duck soup rather than pea soup and I yearned for more challenges.

One of my most satisfying experiences was sailing up Vineyard Sound from Falmouth, Massachusetts, to Quick's Hole in dense fog. The tide was running hard and the wind was on our nose. Tide and current calculations, leeway, and courses made good were all automatic for me by this time. I was totally relaxed for the trip, read a book, and only looked up periodically to check for other boats, blow the horn, or change tacks. I found Quick's Hole just where and when I planned. As we sailed through, the fog lifted and we had a glorious, sunny reach across the bay. A heightened feeling of total confidence and exultation carried me weightless up the hill to our cottage that evening.

With my family growing, we could no longer fit the five of us into the four little bunks of *Little Dove*, so I sold her, not without some regret, and bought a Bristol 32, a design I had admired for years. *Classic* was a truly beautiful boat with sweeping lines, long overhangs, and a traditional appearance. Above all other characteristics, my new boat had to be beautiful. She was a thoroughbred from a standard of CCA Rule boats. No matter that I knew before I bought her that she would be slow. Those lovely long overhangs meant that her waterline length was only twenty-two feet. This was not much longer than our smaller Paceship, which had a nineteen-foot waterline. As boat speed is directly related to the length of the waterline, it turned out that *Classic*'s maximum theoretical speed was only 6.5 knots. *Little Dove*'s was 6.0 knots.

Classic's maiden voyage after some initial sea trials was an offshore two-and-a-half-day trip up to Northeast Harbor, Maine. A new autopilot installed that week decided to steer entirely to starboard, taking us in circles with flogging sails. The wind was rising and when I tried to take over manually, the unit refused to disconnect. This was, of course, at midnight. We doused sails and I spent the next two hours upside down in a cockpit locker taking the autopilot out of the boat. It went back to the factory as soon as we hit shore. The rest of the trip was a dream come true. Crisp, sunny days; brightly colored, trim little cottages and stately mansions nestled among forests of pine; gorgeous sunsets; and a sunrise mirrored on a motionless harbor; all whetted my taste for coastal exploration. Elizabeth, fourteen at the time, spent those two weeks in the forepeak, curled up like a cat. She actually succeeded in reading a dozen books on the trip, the first time she had ever done any reading outside of school. She, of course, scarcely saw Maine and yet, amazingly enough, has turned into a fine and sometimes enthusiastic sailor. Although she often did not participate, she always watched. Nothing escaped her sharp eye. Later, when we went to Nova Scotia, she suddenly pitched in, took tricks at the helm, hauled on winches, delighted in working up the mast in the rigging, and did everything possible to belie her earlier years of disinterest.

The decision to sail transatlantic began as the dream of a five-year-old boy. This youngster who summered with his family in Rockport, Massachusetts, at a time when Rockport was a quiet summer spot, fishing village, and artist community, would gaze at the marine traffic working its way up and down the coast. I clearly recall the schooners that plied that coast in the early 1940s. A significant fleet of vessels working under sail existed in those days. Their magnificent expanse of canvas spread before the wind stimulated my dreams of exploration to far-off places. The magic of Europe lay beyond the horizon just over there. Perhaps, some day . . .

The streets of Rockport were not cluttered with tourists in those days. It was a sleepy little village with one main street and some surrounding farms, woods, and a few isolated houses. The deep diaphone of the foghorn would lull me to sleep every misty night, and when I got back home the next fall, it seemed weeks before I could fall asleep without that deep-voiced friend. My mom and Aunt Jen would take me and my older cousin, Frank, to the beach just seaward of Main Street and we would build castles, and climb over rocks, and forever immerse ourselves in the living wonders of the tide pools. I have kept with me two clear memories of those years. My uncle, Iver Rose, was a well-known artist of the time and he forever painted somber tragedies of ships struggling through storms at sea. His other favorite subject was clowns with their pants falling down. Apparently I was the inspiration, because at the age of three I had no hips to hold up my bathing suit.

In 1980 my first real test presented itself. I wanted to sail offshore and Bermuda, a jewel of a semitropical island, seemed the perfect challenge. One week would be needed to get there, one week to get home, and we would have two glorious weeks of sunlit cruising in Bermuda waters. We left in early June and caught some of the roughest weather in years.

Our trip across was uncomfortable and punctuated by two gales at sea. We fixed our safety harnesses to jacklines strung the length of the boat, and the strict use of those harnesses barely kept everyone aboard. At 5:15 A.M. on the fourth day, we had winds of fifty knots, with sustained gusts even higher. As the storm advanced, I crept onto the deck to put a third reef in the mainsail. While hauling in the reef, I was struck by a large wave that swept across the cabin, striking me with chest-deep water, tearing me from the mast, and flinging me overboard in an instant. My harness was secured to a jackline at the mast and I came up hard against the line and grasped the shrouds. A moment later the ship rolled, and I was lying up against the rail, battered, wet, and scared. Wayne and Al were both shipmates in this early, offshore adventure.

The return trip was even more frightening. We sailed into a huge weather front that spawned an extratropical cyclone of hurricane force that almost destroyed our boat. Huge thirty-five-foot seas built with screaming winds and chattering rigging. The noise was horrendous and the motion of the boat even worse. Attempting to run off under bare poles before the wind, we would rise on one of the monstrous seas and then free-fall down the side of the steep precipice, landing at the bottom with a crash that shook the ship so that I seriously questioned her continuing integrity. Protected in our bunks behind lee cloths, Dave, Bert, and I lay as still as we could, hoping that the monster outside would not see us and would go away. Seasickness took full command of our ship, and efforts at managing her were useless. We simply survived until the center of the storm passed over us.

When the howling of the wind abated and silence crept over the boat, I crawled into the cockpit and saw, for the first time, the eye of a hurricane. Dark, black, rolling clouds seethed in a circle around us about three miles or so in each direction from our position on the epicenter. The night sky was perforated with millions of crystal clear, perfectly formed stars, each standing out against the perfect background of the heavens. It was like being blasted into outer space. The lowered pressure within the storm cleared out all the distorting atmosphere above. I called Dave out to have a look. With awe we realized that we had to go back into the storm. It was all around us and the moment's respite was but that, only a moment. With book-learned knowledge that the western part of a hurricane is the navigable side, we headed due west. In the northern hemisphere, hurricanes spin in a clockwise direction when viewed from above. The storms tend to move in a northeasterly direction and the speed of the storm's movement, which can be from fifteen to fifty miles an hour, is added to the wind speed of the swirling winds if one is so unfortunate as to be in the northeastern corner of the storm. The speed of the storm's movement, on the other hand, is subtracted from the circular force of the winds if one is on the western side of the storm center.

Thus, we survived; we encountered wind speeds of only sixty-five knots on the navigable side of the storm, and we were finally left with slatting sails in a high-pressure system with no wind at all.

The trip to Bermuda had shown me the power of the sea. My beautiful *Classic* with her narrow beam, long overhangs, and sleek lines was too cramped for comfort, and too tender (lay over too easily) for any kind of offshore living. Even in a moderate breeze she would heel over to about thirty degrees. Have you ever tried to put on a pair of pants on a tilted platform that irregularly lurches, dips, and disappears from beneath your feet? As it was, we learned survival. If you wanted to put on your pants, you would simply hold on while others pried and pulled and hauled. Occasionally, the entire crew would end up in a pile of arms and legs, laughing hysterically while the poor, cold, wet, exhausted person at the wheel would grumble about the clowns on the off-watch.

My decision to sell her came the day I was catapulted out of the head from a sitting position through the closed door, breaking off the lock. I was thrown onto the opposite cabin wall. The ignominiousness of being caught thus with my pants down (so to speak) in front of my crass crew, who had the nerve to literally scream with laughter, was the final straw. *Classic*, thirty-two feet in length and 11,400 pounds displacement, had seemed huge when I bought her, but had become quite tiny on the big ocean. If I was going to do any more blue water sailing, I required a sturdier craft.

Thus the search for a fully found, stiff, able, comfortable, and seaworthy sailing ship began. My desire was to have a vessel with traditional lines above the waterline and a modern underwater configuration. A New England boatbuilder was chosen. The process of construction, testing, preparation, and fine-tuning began in January of 1981. Construction was completed on August 1, and we set off for a shakedown cruise to Nova Scotia shortly after launch.

Our trip to Lunenburg, Nova Scotia, and thence to Mahone Bay and Halifax, was blessed with fine weather and clear sailing. We developed an understanding of our new, fine vessel and were convinced that she could meet any weather. It was during this trip that sailing started to appeal to Cindy in a new way. "The new yacht gave me a feeling of confidence and comfort. It was large enough and built well enough to relieve many of my past worries. Meanwhile, somehow when we weren't looking, the children had grown up. Now Bob and I weren't sailing with three little kids; the older two were self-sufficient and could carry their own load. This made it easier for me to begin to enjoy sailing rather than worrying about my young children and their needs."

That winter, I had *Free Spirit* surveyed by a savvy old captain from Marblehead. Despite her admirable construction, he pointed out several areas that needed attention to make her safe for an ocean passage: One of the starboard water tanks needed additional blocking to keep it firmly in place, the battery boxes had to be secured to prevent the batteries from tipping out, and the gussets in the starboard chainplates needed strengthening. The propane locker should be sealed, and several minor items required repair.

Work was begun in a local shipyard and was completed by spring. After some discussion about outrageous fees with the smooth con man at the yard, I reached a compromise with him. This was an adventure in itself. All winter I had received regular bills from the yard; by May they totaled $7,000. Detailed and graphic descriptions of the work done accompanied each invoice. I paid each promptly. Suddenly, in early May, I received a $10,000 invoice. I looked at it and it seemed to include all the work I had ordered. *Free Spirit* was launched and rigged, and I assumed that this was the final bill. I figured that I was being overcharged about $5,000, but since I had not insisted on a price beforehand, it was my own fault. I paid the bill. You can imagine how I felt two weeks later when I was handed another bill for $10,000. I called my surveyor the Marblehead captain, and he said, "It sounds like you're being taken over the coals." That weekend I asked him to meet me on the boat and arranged, in advance, to take the boat out on a trial sail—so he could clear her survey for insurance purposes. We sailed to a nearby harbor and tied up. He went over all the invoices and toted up his estimate of what the job should cost. We were being taken advantage of, and badly. I simply did not return to the yard. We sailed up to Boston and I called the yard and told them that I had lost confidence in their ability to provide work at a reasonable cost. I later consulted an expert from Connecticut, a former manager of a New York boatyard and a builder of America's Cup boats. I still had to pay a significant bill (the compromise), which seriously damaged my cruising kitty, but I had the yard off my back and eliminated any potential legal problems for the future. As my lawyer pointed out, in spite of the fact that I had obtained two independent surveyors' written testimony that the work should not have cost over $17,000 at the outside, the yard owner would simply appear in court in coveralls, toting pages of time cards, and intimating that the rich doctor/yacht owner could afford the bills. No information would come out in court that the yard owner was a multimillionaire who owned his own sixty-five-foot yacht. I was the sucker and I got suckered. At least I was able to keep the damage under control.

With *Free Spirit* ready, it was time to focus on other aspects of our transatlantic odyssey. Preparation for a major ocean passage requires intense forethought and planning.

Professionally, I had made provision to take significant time off. Five years earlier, I had taken on an associate in my medical practice. With a partner, I could leave on an extended voyage knowing I would have something to return to.

Charts had to be obtained not only for the crossing but for the coasts we planned to cruise, and local charts for out-of-the-way places can be difficult to obtain. I spent months organizing this part of the trip. With perhaps three hundred ocean, coastal, and harbor charts covering the Atlantic, Ireland, Norway, Scotland, England, Denmark, Germany, Holland, France, Spain, Portugal, and the Azores, a complete list of our charts, and orderly storage, were essential.

Advance plotting allowed me to discover a serious error in the Hydrographic Service's chart of Florø, Norway, and environs. The magnetic variation on the compass rose of the chart was off by fifteen degrees, a fact that I pointed out in a letter to the service. If I had picked up the chart at the last minute while en route, we probably would have missed that error and might have been set on the rocks in the storm that struck us there.

Last-minute shopping for the carefully planned food supplies and other necessities for the four months we were to be away resulted in the largest single order ever to be placed at Roche Brothers Supermarket in Wellesley. The bill came to $1,200 in 1982 dollars and the haul lowered the waterline of *Free Spirit* by a full six inches.

Since both Cindy and I work full time, I usually do most of the shopping for the family because I generally get home earlier than she does. Thus I had a pretty good idea how much of everything we tended to use in a week. I simply walked into the supermarket and started pulling things off the shelves. I had the manager get me cases of items such as soda that I would need in volume. We filled seventeen shopping carts with supplies, loaded them into a large trailer, and took it all down to the boat early the next morning. Cindy helped me transfer the stuff to the dock. The cartons stretched in three rows from one end of *Free Spirit* to the other. Cindy, with her usual cautious view, held that there was no way that we could get all that stuff aboard. I sent her off to work and started packing. Things went into cupboards, below the floors, and into wet lockers. Any spot where there was the possibility of storage received its share. I finally got it all aboard. *Free Spirit* was well below her designed waterline even without any people or their personal gear aboard.

An adventure at sea can be an uplifting and exhilarating experience, but illness or injury can turn it into hell. The preparation of a complete medical kit is a vital part of any long-distance voyager's obligation. The sailor becomes exhausted easily in his first days at sea, he may incur an injury, and seasickness is a distinct possibility. Also, one is no less susceptible to the development of illness at sea than on land, with the added complication that delay in obtaining medical help could lead to a tragedy. Furthermore, the farther off the beaten track a cruise takes you, the less likelihood of finding expertise to assist in managing illness or injury.

In our case, my profession made assembly of our medical supplies a simple matter. For the layman, consultation with a physician and study of a good book on first aid at sea are essential. Appendix C lists the contents of our medical kit for the journey. With advance preparation and knowledge, most illnesses and injuries become routine and easy to care for, and one can relax, confident that everything is under control. This confidence translates into clear decisions and early and appropriate treatment.

While certain medications and supplies such as intravenous fluids should only be carried by a medical professional, many prescription drugs should be carried, for example antibiotics, and medications for asthma, diarrhea, ulcers, sea sickness, and allergies. You should acquire information regarding appropriateness and method of their use by careful research and a thorough discussion with your doctor, from whom you must get all prescriptions. A detailed medical kit list is included in the appendix; it can be supplemented as required in consultation with your doctor.

After ten days in Nantucket, rested and refreshed, with a replacement for Wayne aboard, and supplies replenished, we were ready again to launch our journey. We had originally planned on a brief stop in the Azores, but now we determined to head straight for Ireland. We would follow the great circle course, skirting the edges of the Newfoundland Grand Banks, and head for Fastnet Rock. We sailed on June twenty-fourth.

CHAPTER 3

Nantucket Embarkation

With windblown spray
   and angry gray
You teach humility.

Cross storm-bred seas
'neath seething clouds
we drive on endlessly.

*W*e're off—*again*. The twenty-fourth day of June 1982 was an absolutely beautiful day, sunny and cool, with light breezes and a flat, calm sea. What a temptress she is. Lulled into complacency, we had hot roast beef sandwiches for supper. Dolphins came to visit us and played in our bow wave, much to our delight. If that wasn't enough of a thrill, we saw our first whale blow. I was smitten. And to think I was ready to give it all up.

We sailed easily along under twin running sails on a downwind reach. Watch-keeping was rough on the skipper that first night. I was up with all shifts: up with Peter to set the main to ease the rolling; up with Elizabeth to explain the use of and the methodology behind the dead reckoning log; up with Al and Elizabeth to replace the twin running sail halyard, which had parted after chafing on the rough edge of the radar dome. This halyard had laid against the edge of the radar dome. As the sail pulled and eased with the roll of the boat, the halyard was pulled back and forth against this relatively sharp edge. Sawed through, the halyard parted and the sail came floating down onto the deck. Here, Elizabeth was to prove her value. The only one on board who was totally unafraid of heights, she thoroughly enjoyed being hauled to the masthead. She would kick off the mast and swing herself around the entire stick. We hoisted her to the running block for the twins and she threaded a new halyard. This she accomplished with *Free Spirit* rolling along at six knots in four- to six-foot seas. Lashings pulled it away from the radar to keep it from further chafe until a permanent repair could be fashioned in Europe.

We had a good breakfast the next morning—hot cereal, freshly baked blueberry muffins, and orange juice. Laughter bubbled about the galley. Slowly working her way along under light winds and the twins, *Free Spirit* was stately that day. The twin running sails are attached to a common luff wire leading from the bow of the boat to a point near the top of the mast. The two sails are poled out onto two wooden whisker poles set on their own track on the mast. For such downwind work, they are a lot easier to use than a spinnaker on a boat the size of *Free Spirit* and require minimal handling once set. On a roller-furling drum, they can be set or furled in a matter of moments. In a half a gale, they can be partially furled to run as a reefed downwind rig.

It was hot and sunny at noon and I was in shorts. What a difference a couple of weeks makes. Near six in the evening, the breeze came in from the southwest at an estimated twelve to fifteen knots. Reaching along with the mainsail and twins we were now doing six knots. I took my first set of sights since the Bermuda trip two years earlier, and found that I was twenty-two miles off the SatNav reading. I guess I was a bit rusty. Frankly, after all that time off I was happy to find myself in the right ocean!

The satellite navigator is a wonderful electronic tool that depends on an intrinsic computer and radio receiver picking up satellite communications to estimate the boat's position. The SatNav receives signals sent from any one of a number of satellites that the U.S. government has placed in orbit to improve navigation for the navy. Using an analogous process to the Doppler principle, whereby a sound changes pitch as the object creating the sound passes by the listener, the receiver on board can determine when a satellite has passed overhead. Since the computer is able to recognize the satellite by a code and since the satellite's position over the earth is known (and in the computer's memory bank), the position of the boat relative to the satellite can then be determined. Its value cannot be overstated. Today, no ship should go to sea without this vital piece of equipment.

Al and the kids played Dungeons and Dragons all afternoon and after dinner they moved on to Cosmic Wimpout. Five feet ten inches tall, thin and wiry, with wavy black hair and a trim little mustache, Al had a quick smile and was most cooperative. He had been an extremely valuable and pleasant crewmate on my sail to Bermuda, with his fine sense of humor and easy manner. Most of his sailing to this point had been on family cruises in New England waters and, except for our Bermuda trip, this was to be his first major deep-water adventure.

I polished the chrome ventilators and resealed the leaky chainplates, which naturally always leaked onto the skipper's bunk.

On board, everyone was given responsibilities geared to skills, ability, and experience. I plotted positions on the chart with the aid of the SatNav and kept a dead-reckoning log, a position estimated by course and speed. Each of the kids and Cindy eventually learned to do these chores, too. At least once a day I tried to take celestial sightings to confirm our position unless clouds, fog, or seasickness intervened. I also did much of the cooking, since I like to eat well. I tried to bake muffins in the morning and gave everyone a good breakfast. Eggs, obtained from a local farm before we left, had been coated with vaseline to keep them fresh and were stored unrefrigerated. (The vaseline seals the eggshell and helps to keep the interior bacteria-free. Once a week we turned them, which helped preserve them.) Evening meals either came out of the freezer and were warmed on the stove or, if conditions warranted, were prepared from scratch. Lunches were usually prepared by Cindy or Elizabeth. We had one rule: Whoever prepared a meal did not have to clean up afterward. Cleanup duties were evenly spread among Cindy, Al, and the kids. Every day the head (toilet area) had to be cleaned and this duty rotated among all aboard. And everyone shared in keeping the boat shipshape.

The following day was the same—sunny skies and moderate winds from the south-southeast. We carried on under yankee and mainsail. All of us enjoyed getting into Cosmic Wimpout, a delightfully idiotic game brought along by Al. We played Dodgem with a number of fishing boats on the Banks that night and Cindy took most of the after-midnight watches. We made it a practice in all kinds of weather to have the person on watch go out into the cockpit every ten minutes to scan the entire horizon for signs of other boats. If any appeared, the watch was to call me. After a week or so, the rest of the crew learned to make their own judgments and I was called less often. In fog, we used the radar for watches, turning on the scanner every ten minutes by our kitchen timer.

The food so far had worked out well. I baked a carrot and spice cake for the late watch, and then started to teach Peter and Cindy the rudiments of celestial navigation. This was the first time I had used the H.O. 249 sight reduction tables for air navigation. Previously I had used an electronic calculator programmed for celestial, but for this trip I wanted to be independent of anything electrical in case our other systems went down. The technique is straightforward enough. If you know where the sun is at any particular moment of a particular day (obtained from a publication called the nautical almanac) and you have a rough idea of where you are, you can measure the angle of the sun from the horizon. If the sun were directly overhead, it would measure ninety degrees. The farther you are away from the sun, the smaller is the angle that you measure. Thus, the angle that you measure gives you the distance that you are from a point on the earth directly beneath the sun. Since you have tables that tell you just where the sun is, you then know how far you are from this point. This will give you a line of position. This line of position is measured from the known position of the sun at that time of day. This is similar in concept to taking a line of position from a headland or an island. It tells you approximately where you are. In order to get a better fix, you need to get a second line of position from something else—another headland, or tower, or island. Crossing the two lines of position gives you a reasonably accurate position fix. In celestial navigation, one either compares the position of the sun with some other celestial body such as the moon, or compares it with the position of the sun later in the day (called a running fix). A few simple formulas, a couple of tables in some books, a steady eye with the sextant, an accurate watch, and some common sense and you can find your way anywhere. The H.O. 249 tables are generally preferred for small-boat navigation to the more cumbersome H.O. 229 (the same tables for marine navigation) because they are easier to use and have fewer steps. The slight decrease in accuracy is undetectable in a small boat at sea.

Four days out, the wind drew around to forward of our beam and we dropped our twin running sails, which had been up almost from the start. The sky was becoming overcast and a weak front moved through, with light rain followed by fog. The wind shifted back to the southwest and we put the twins back up and drifted along at four knots. *Free Spirit* rose and fell to the swell. I spoke by radio with a German tanker that spotted us on radar at seven miles. It was very comforting to have him verify that we could be seen.

That night, we lost all wind, the sails began to flog back and forth with the rolling of the boat, and we had to take down all sail. To try to diminish the extent of the roll, we elected to motor with the storm trysail sheeted in tight. This proved to be more successful than using the main, as we could then tie down the boom, which otherwise was crashing back and forth, shaking the rig mightily. Dense fog descended on our little world that night, so we kept a radar watch as well as a visual watch.

Elizabeth recalled the night watches with mixed feelings. "I hated going on watch, putting on foul-weather gear and going out in the cold. I remember that the first time I was on watch late at night, I fell asleep. Dad woke me up at three in the morning, yelled at me, and told me that I could be responsible for the death of the whole family.

This really sank in because I could see that it was true. However, I still found it hard to stay awake. I used to take the timer out with me and set it every ten minutes so that I would wake up and look around. Sometimes I read, not for enjoyment but just to stay awake. After about two weeks at sea, it got to the point that we had a routine. It was as if I had done it all my life and I could go on doing it forever. I stopped being bored with being at sea. Dad taught me celestial navigation and how to use the SatNav and radar. It was all so interesting when I had a chance to apply what I was learning."

Peter also remembered those early days. "Everyone was sick in the beginning, but it was a great feeling when we got our sea legs. I felt that I could do anything. I was horrified when Elizabeth fell asleep on watch. I was so mad at her, and then, two nights later, it happened to me. We would get so tired at night. I would sit at the desk where all the navigation instruments and charts were kept with the little red nightlight on giving an eerie glow to the cabin. It was so lonely with everybody asleep. I really felt isolated with the ship charging along, everything in blackness but that little red glow. The noise of the seas and the creaking of the mast and the pounding of the ship sometimes made it sound as if someone had boarded us and was walking around on deck. A block would scrape on the deck, a line flutter, some piece of gear move; then when I would go topside to take a look, all I could see were the green or red of our bow light on the foam and the dark shape of our foredeck, the dinghy lashed there, sails drawing cleanly.

"Outside, it was invigorating, but always a shock at first. With the ship leaping over the seas, with the wind in my face, spray covering the foredeck, I felt so adventurous, like a conqueror, as if I was on top of the world.

"I'll tell you one thing that you shouldn't do though, and that is read scary stories. I read *Lord of the Flies* at night and with all the noises, the dark, and the loneliness, it was really overpowering. One thing I never got used to was the whine of the radar. Our unit had a high-pitched squeal and it was awful when everything else was quiet.

"This trip marked the first time that we kids had gotten along well. It had something to do with sharing a load and having to work together just to survive."

June twenty-eighth we celebrated Cindy's birthday in style. Elizabeth baked a birthday cake, and we passed around party hats. After a brisket and noodle pudding we had cake and ice cream, and "Happy Birthday" sung in at least three different keys.

On the twenty-ninth, I was up with Elizabeth for much of her one to three in the morning watch. With the eerie fog and the circle of darkness surrounding our lonely craft, her sixteen years began to show as her imagination invented all sorts of creatures to inhabit the darkness. We sang some songs together and then furled the main to ease the degree of heel, leaving only the yankee up to drive us along at our hull speed of eight knots while we curled up together in the cockpit.

The following day we found that we had a leak between the anchor locker in the forepeak and the forward berth. Little John was the only one small enough to fit inside the locker, and he sealed it for us with epoxy. The new responsiveness of our craft resulted in some queasiness all around. John remembers, "I felt so important that day. I was the only one little enough to crawl inside the locker to seal it. I always looked up to Peter. He was my older brother. I'd do anything to be like him. I really wanted him to notice me and not blow me off. He noticed that day."

* * *

Free Spirit is a Mariner 47, built to our specifications by the Mariner Yacht Company of East Rochester, New Hampshire. With a traditional trunk cabin and a modest overhang fore and aft, a long cruising fin keel with only six feet of draft, and a separate skeg-hung rudder, she was strongly built and, with her 32,000 pounds of displacement, was able to stand up to the seas and a good breeze quite well. Boasting a gleaming white hull and ample varnished brightwork, a powerful sloop rig modified to a cutter by the addition of a staysail on a running stay, she made a pretty picture as she charged through the sun-flecked foam.

With *Little Dove* and *Classic* behind us, we wanted a boat that would give us strength and stability to stand up to heavy seas, and enough waterline length to be able to sail at eight knots or better. We still wanted classic looks but were willing to compromise here for improved speed and stability. I went out on test sails on a number of different boats. The O.C. 40 and the Alden 44 had similar handling characteristics to *Classic*. They heeled easily and bounced lightly on the waves. The Bristol 45.5 was a different story. With 36,000 pounds of displacement, she moved through the water with grace and power. She seemed to part the waters and to be unaffected by small seas. I loved the feel, but I didn't like the looks. She appeared to be cut off at the stern as if she had been meant to be a longer vessel. I continued to search. Then I saw her. In a sailing magazine there was a profile of a handsome-looking yacht, a Mariner. I drove to New Hampshire to see hull #1, which had just been launched. I was smitten. The next month I flew down to Annapolis to sail her as she was in the Annapolis sailboat show. She was light on the helm and a joy to sail, a big boat with the same handling characteristics as the Bristol 45.5. She moved through the water with authority, and she had a solid, bolted-on lead keel that would be able to withstand a grounding if necessary. In spite of the shaky financial status of the builder, I made a deposit on a new Mariner 47.

Cindy and I worked long hours that winter designing and redesigning the interior to meet our needs. We ended up with a beautiful boat that lived up to most of our expectations.

On the thirtieth of June, we fled south in response to a high seas forecast the night before. A North Atlantic gale warning was broadcast, with the gale center expected to be over New York State at noon, moving northeast. The winds blew about forty knots and we drove along under the diminutive area of a reefed mainsail at eight knots. Everyone was seasick from the difficult motion. This was the first day that I spent entirely in my bunk, except for one sail change to a deeply reefed genoa with storm staysail and reefed main. I chose this combination to balance the helm better and ease the strain on the autopilot. We elected to run south from the storm all night. No watches were kept. We were all too sick.

July first found us charging across the vast emptiness of the open Atlantic, oblivious to our course, vaguely headed toward Ireland, and scarcely caring whom or what we might meet. We sent out security calls on our VHF at erratic intervals, advising all shipping of our headlong rush to potential disaster. We were interested only in crawling into a warm sleeping bag to thaw our freezing feet, lying down, and trying to stay the curse of the sea. The sky was gray and overcast, with visibility a half mile or so in fog, haze, and a light drizzle. The seas were six to eight feet—nothing dangerous, but dizzying in their irregular blows to our senses. The wind was out of the south at twenty knots. I finally got up and had an English muffin and coffee, and served some hot chocolate and muffins to the crew. All were bedridden at this point except Al and me. I washed up and shaved, changed clothes, and felt great. Then I brushed my teeth and promptly lost my lunch. At this point, I was beginning to have a pretty good idea why so few people sail across the Atlantic. We were at this time 158 miles from the Grand Banks of Newfoundland, which we were to skirt before taking our great circle course to Ireland. Thank God for the SatNav. It was a lifesaver. At least we always knew just about where we were.

My log for July second reads: "Oh what a rotten night last night was. I was ready to quit—truly quit, sell the boat, go home. If I could have had someone pluck me out of this bucking, rolling horror I would have done so." The wind had died and left us slatting and rolling in large swells. We tried to motor into it with a reefed mainsail up, but we couldn't take the motion below. I became so sick! After two or three hours, I struggled out of bed, set full sail, and strapped her in. This helped to ease the motion. We were again headed northeast toward Ireland.

I lay back down in my bunk and cuddled with my wife. She moaned in response. I thought, why am I doing this? What is it I hope to accomplish? The answer eluded me as I drifted off into slumber. I was too tired for philosophical discussions with myself that night.

We continued to motor for waypoint one, the Grand Banks. We had spoken to a tanker that morning. We raised him on the radio and he said he'd keep an eye out for us.

He was near us on our port side and catching up to us at 30.5 knots! That's scary.

Half a cup of ice cold milk and three pretzels put me in shape for the next day. Amazing—an otherwise awful breakfast, but it was the only thing I felt I could keep down. Peter was up at last and did some calisthenics. He felt as limp as a rag after spending the last twenty-four hours in bed. By eleven-thirty everyone was up and more or less functioning. We were at that point sailing well on a close reach. It was cloudy, cool, and raw. We kept five-minute radar watches. The highlight of the morning was an all-crew rendition of "Dona Nobis Pacem" in harmony. Peter kept us in stitches in the beginning because he couldn't sing on key with his changing voice. We tried to raise other shipping on the VHF radio, but obviously no one was within the fifty-mile transmitting range of our antenna. We sang songs to the world, feeling silly and giddy, delighted we were all alive and no longer ill.

That day was pleasant and quiet. The seas were subsiding, the wind mild, and there was fog. It could have been worse. We perked up the crew with barbecued chicken for dinner that night. Cindy and I had precooked a number of such meals at home, freezing them for later re-creation at sea. Roast pork, lasagne, beef stroganoff, pizza, and Chinese food were all part of our frozen stock of reminders of home. They helped to spark renewed vigor and enthusiasm when things looked bleakest.

July third was sunny, cool, and calm. Odd jobs and leaks to be repaired filled our day. Mattresses and sleeping bags were dragged out to be dried. We made BLTs and potato salad for lunch and that afternoon I baked bread for the first time.

Independence day proved beautiful and sunny, with high,

thin clouds, after the fog lifted at 9:00 A.M. Moderate fifteen-knot winds from our starboard quarter gave us an easy run at six knots under main and genoa. We celebrated the Fourth with all-American hamburgers cooked by Elizabeth. Next came a rousing rendition of "The Star-Spangled Banner" by the crew in the cockpit. (Al was particularly patriotic, standing at attention with his hand over his heart.) The finale? Fireworks, of course: We fired the ship's shotgun. Cindy and Elizabeth plugged their ears.

Our next gale at sea hit us on the fifth. Winds of twenty-five knots increased to forty knots. Seas gradually built to twenty feet or so and we started to surf down the big ones, at times reaching twelve knots on our speedometer and twice pegging out at eighteen knots.

We did 200 miles that day, averaging 8.33 knots. *Free Spirit* handled the big seas with aplomb and her crew actually enjoyed this test of weather. For Cindy and the kids, this relatively benign storm was the highlight of our crossing, our first real test as a sailing crew. No one was sick or scared. We all had our sea legs. The wind, although powerful, was relatively warm. We all took turns at the wheel, surfing down the big seas and laughing as we found our big yacht handling like a sailing dinghy. What a blast!

One of the most interesting aspects of the passage was the effect it had on relationships among the kids. Peter and Elizabeth, no longer free to find other friends, had to rely on each other for friendship and support. I began to notice improving cooperation between them and few, if any, of their usual spats. Cindy and I were accustomed to helping each other over the rough spots, and did so. John bubbled along with no worries about anything except a peculiar mutual barrage of minor insults with Al. Al, getting along fine with the rest of the crew, seemed to enjoy baiting little John. Our youngest seemed to take it all in stride and I saw no need to intervene. Eventually, Cindy and I quietly took Al aside and asked him to ease up on the teasing.

Cindy noted that the limited space and small accommodations available in a boat at sea forced neatness and cooperation on all of us. There was simply no room aboard for thrown clothes or gear. Wet clothes were hung in the engine compartment to dry or were strung on temporary lines throughout the boat. As soon as they were dry, they were put away, to be periodically replaced on the lines with other soggy garments. Existence at sea mandated cooperation, working together for our mutual well-being. This left little room for dumb pranks. Shipping, fog, rain, sail changes, ship repairs, watches, navigation—all were at the forefront of our attention. Petty jealousies, ill humor, and selfish preoccupations had to take a backseat.

On the sixth of July, we passed the halfway point. We found ourselves 1,256.5 nautical miles distant from Ireland and with 1,269.4 nautical miles under our keel. Talk about being in the middle of nowhere! No radio messages, no ships, nothing, except an English language broadcast we could pick up from England. It felt strange sitting out there. I thought back to the times as a youngster when I sat on the rocks of Rockport harbor, dreaming about what it would be like to cross the great Atlantic ocean. Who would have believed that I would actually do it on my own boat?

CHAPTER 4

Midocean Madness

*M*idocean is a strange place for civilized man. Nothing but sea and sky can be seen. The ship rushes and plunges, lifting her bow to throw off a sea and then diving again as if to see what's below the surface. Waves, marching in ranks and platoons, come in all shapes and sizes, none the same. One will curl over and play dead while another leaps over a neighbor in playful exuberance. Yet it is a march of a dead army. You can yell and they don't hear you. You can cry; they march along. You could drown beneath their feet and they would pay no heed. Rising from the cradle near coasts far away and marching to a grave we know not where—and God save the poor soul who gets in their inexorable way.

Above, the sun or the stars, it matters not. They look down, watching over us with unseeing eyes. Are we on earth? Is this really our home? Or have we been flung off the planet in our rush across the sea to find ourselves drifting aimlessly forever?

* * *

Radio was no help. All we could hear was static, with occasional bursts of strange music or incomprehensible speech, perhaps Portuguese or Spanish, and once or twice a familiar name, "Presidente Reagan" or "America." The voice of Israel reached us for five minutes or so before drifting off into oblivion. An English-language version of the voice of the Soviet Union soothingly sold its message. But mostly nothing, only static and Morse code and the wash of the seas, the crash of the bow, the creaking of the mast. Everything was suddenly still and silent and I felt totally alone. I awakened and looked about at my sleeping crew. Al was huddled in his sleeping bag, his little mustache rising and falling quietly with each breath. The others were merely shadows. The timer rang and I slowly and reluctantly rose to drag myself to the companionway. I opened it up and slipped outside to shiver in the gloom.

Prior to the trip Cindy had a great deal of difficulty visualizing thousands of miles of open ocean. She had an unreasoning fear of 360° of horizon. While still at home, she would try to picture this while driving to work on Route 128. It made her break out into a cold sweat. Actually, she found that being able to see the horizon was not terrifying, but reassuring. It was when she couldn't see that she was frightened. Much of the early part of our trip, especially as we approached the Grand Banks of Newfoundland, was spent shrouded in fog. We would plunge headlong through the mist both day and night, relying on our imperfect sense of hearing and an electronic marvel, radar, that we didn't fully trust. "I felt as if I was running at full speed along a crowded highway with my eyes blindfolded!" Cindy recalled later. "It was simply terrifying to race forward in a thirty-two-thousand-pound sailboat with the knowledge that somewhere out there were tankers and container ships, the only things that could destroy us, swift, ocean-going monsters weighing thousands of tons.

"I never really got my sea legs. I am always full of energy at home. I do aerobic exercises every day. On the boat, my energy level seemed to diminish. It was as if my tank was on empty. I tried to help out, but all I could do was stand watches. I was better in the cockpit, and absolutely helpless in the cabin. Often I would find myself lying in my bunk, disabled by dizziness and weakness, listening to Bob and Peter on deck. I would hear everything magnified: bumps, raps, grating sounds as various jobs were done topsides. It petrified me that they were on deck in bad weather and I was stuck below. If anything bad happened and they went over the side, I could have done nothing to help them. It seemed to take forever for them to do anything. Although I knew that Bob worked slowly and methodically while on deck to avoid making a mistake, it always seemed as if something must have gone wrong for him to be taking so much time.

"Night sailing itself never bothered me. If the visibility was good, a moon might be out, stars could be seen, the horizon was always there, and you could see where you were going. It was only when haze or fog settled in, sometimes imperceptibly, and you were never sure of what else was out there."

John had his own personal fears: "I felt a lot of fear before the trip, but I didn't show it because my brother and sister didn't. Ever since *Little Dove*, I've been afraid of big waves and being out of control. This probably was because I was so little then." Indeed, John began sailing while he was two and he certainly shared some of our early experiences with wild thrashes to weather crossing Buzzard's Bay. Some of it must have been terrifying to a little kid. When the weather got bad, he would sing a little ditty over and over about how he loved the boat. "Oh *Little Dove,* oh, *Little Dove,* oh *Little Dove,* how I love you." On this trip he was afraid that something would happen and there would be no one around to help, or that I would go overboard, and then no one could take care of the ship.

Fear has a way of paralyzing the soul. It becomes pervasive, leaves one's skin cold, mouth dry, and temper short. Worst of all, when you are in charge of a little boat, with all aboard trusting in your judgment, your competence, and your sanity, such unease is not something you can share with your companions.

Roughly halfway across the Atlantic, with 1200 nautical miles separating our craft from the weather station in Norfolk, Virginia, I was struck with a most overwhelming fear—a kind of terror I had never experienced before.

When sailing on the open ocean, there is a certain expectation of bad weather. We were certainly well prepared. A strong, seaworthy, carefully surveyed vessel and new storm sails somewhat made up for our light weight and inexperienced crew. In the previous storm, we had used the weather bureau's storm parameters to chart a course due south to avoid the worst of the system and thus had an exhilarating experience with forty-knot winds and twenty-foot seas, entirely reasonable for our forty-seven-foot vessel.

This time we received a warning that a new storm was tracking across New York and was expected to head our way. We counted on getting an update the next night at 9:00 P.M. local time. By then we had drawn farther from the station's source, so when the report started, it came in a staccato of latitudes and longitudes with garbled static in between. As the crucial moment arrived, Cindy erupted into the cabin from the cockpit. "Bob, come on deck, now!"

she shouted. "We are about to hit a sailboat." I leaped out on deck. The boat was charging through the black with occasional glimpses of frothy whiteness in her jaws. The moon was breaking out of the clouds onto the horizon ahead. The luminescent, orange spinnaker Cindy was sure she saw was only that luminescent moon, peeking above the waves.

Later, Cindy would be barraged with jokes about her spinnaker on the horizon. At the moment, however, I had a more immediate concern. In responding to her frantic summons, I had missed the central point of the weather report: the new coordinates of the approaching storm. Winds of sixty knots were forecast for a distance of 300 miles from the storm's center.

Were we about to get clobbered? Vainly, I tried to reach any ship in the area with my VHF radio. Every two hours for the next three days, I broadcast, "To any ship in the vicinity, this is the sailing vessel *Free Spirit*. Please come back." I hoped to be able to get a weather update. For three days, this message was broadcast, over and over. For three days, we received no response. For the first time, I realized just how alone we were and all my determination to control my destiny flew out the companionway. All previous problems successfully solved counted as nothing. What if we were struck by the storm and it was a killer? What then? What if we went down? What if? What if?

In fact, the storm gradually worked its way north and ground itself out over Labrador. Our vessel continued her way peacefully toward the Emerald Isle. I gradually came to grips with the reality that being at sea is really a separation from all the security of civilization. It was a part of my growth as a sailor. It was my rite of passage that summer of 1982.

CHAPTER 5

Landfall

July eighth was a lazy day of sunbathing and reading for the skipper. Al, his mustache twisted in concentration, showed Peter and John how to make a box kite. The challenge of flying the thing without fouling the rigging occupied the afternoon and amused everyone. The ship charged downwind under the twins at an average of 7.5 knots, her broad stern sliding down the large, gentle seas. I placed the barbecue on the port rail and served a charcoal-broiled steak for dinner, complete with rice pilaf and an asparagus-based vegetable concoction of my own devising, eliciting surfeited sighs from everyone. We played hearts again that night and I shot the moon. Everyone now had the bug and tried for all the marbles at least once. The evening was beautiful and clear and we continued to reach downwind. We had 1,048 miles to go, and 1,461 nautical miles under our keel.

The following day dawned cloudy, but gradually cleared. Elizabeth spent some time teaching John math, and read. I worked on sights with Peter and Elizabeth, showing them how to use both the calculator and H.O. 249 for sight reductions. All of us got reasonable sights.

That night, a heater fire almost set aflame the cabinet that housed our furnace. We took the cabinet apart and hosed down the burning wood with a fire extinguisher. We now recognized the kerosene furnace as a serious hazard and it was designated for deep-sixing at the first opportunity. I decided to get a diesel furnace in Europe. Boat maintenance tasks seemed never to end. We exhausted our first tank of propane fuel two weeks into the trip, much sooner than I had expected. I switched to our second tank and immediately smelled the strong odor of propane. Quickly, I shut the tank down and put soap on the connections. Sure enough, one of the connectors leaked— there was no sealing tape on it. I sealed and reconnected it. Not only had the shipyard overcharged me, it had been utterly careless in doing the work. This error could have destroyed our ship and all aboard. They had installed the tanks for me, changing us over from a compressed natural gas system to propane. In order to do so, they were supposed to seal the openings where wiring went through the gas locker. If the regular gas vents had somehow become plugged, the gas would have found its way into the bilge and we might have exploded. I spent the next hour upside down in this locker, sealing all openings with epoxy. This is an experience everyone should try once. With the ship bobbing and weaving like a boxer, my inverted position taught me what it must have been like when the obstetrician hauled me up by my heels and slapped my stern.

Cindy and I decided to alter our course for Baltimore Harbor on the southwest coast of Ireland, because they were reported to have better facilities there than in Bantry Bay, our original destination. The day had been deteriorating, not because of the weather but because Al kept disrespectfully calling me "scupper" instead of skipper. Even the pride of my life, my firstborn, had begun to use that abysmal pseudonym. I wouldn't have minded, but I thought of it first. You'd think that I alone would own the right. Ah, me, the burdens of command.

I must mention one of the chief sacrifices one has to make when traveling with teenagers. If there is to be peace, you must allow them to bring along samples of their music. *Free Spirit* was therefore rent with the discordant rhythms of Led Zeppelin and the Grateful Dead. She vibrated to the beat of Michael Jackson's "Thriller." She curtsyed to the sounds of such luminaries as The Who and Pink Floyd. After the ravages of two weeks at sea, I put my foot down. Fathers have rights to, I insisted. Beethoven, Tchaikovsky, Dvořák, and Grieg replaced the Dead Zeppelin (whatever) some of the time. I thought the ship sailed more easily to such romantic strains, though there were some who disagreed. But wonder of wonders, the kids did eventually seem to develop a taste for classical music.

A 2:00 P.M. celestial sighting placed us within two miles of the SatNav fix. The rigging had loosened up, allowing the mast to work, so we hove to for an hour to adjust it. After tightening each of the turnbuckles on the leeward side, we then switched tacks and were able to do the same on the other.

We all looked forward to a stationary existence. The night before our scheduled landfall, we had a pleasant dinner. The evening was cool and clear, with a good breeze from the stern quarter. Having cooked as usual, I had no cleanup chores and was enjoying an after-dinner stretch in the cockpit while the rest of the crew tripped over each other trying to spruce up the galley and prepare for another night of hearts around the table. This had by now become a regular ritual that we all enjoyed. I got up to scan the horizon. Surely we could all benefit from an early landfall. Suddenly, entirely on impulse, I shouted out so the heavens could hear, "Land hoooo!" The entire crew bounded as one up on deck. Where? Where? What? I lay back on the seat and roared with laughter. "Just kidding," I chuckled. Disgust.

At about five the next morning, Elizabeth, on watch, called out loudly, "Land ho!" Everyone ignored her and turned over, snarling "Shut up and let me sleep," and "It's not funny," and "She thinks she's skipper now." Two hours later, at the change of the watch, we discovered that this time it was no joke. On the morning of July fifteenth, we had finally arrived.

Reaching land marked a turning point in the life of my family. As John said, "With nothing but horizon everywhere for weeks at a time and with no one else out there, you had to get along. We built up a tolerance for each other just like we did for seasickness." Peter was stunned by the reality of what we had done. "It couldn't really be, yet there was this blue land. Back home the land wasn't blue." Elizabeth had more practical things on her mind. "I couldn't wait to take a shower. With my long hair, it was hard for me to wash up, and I'm afraid I used to cheat. Also, I could hardly wait to see the men." Elizabeth would not be disappointed.

The soft, blue gray hills and low mountains of the southwest tip of Ireland were on our port bow. The highlands were gently shrouded in a gossamer mist. An orca, or killer whale, broke the surface in lazy pursuit of who knew what. All around us was clear. We arrived at Fastnet Rock at 10:00 A.M. local time. Al raised the yellow quarantine flag required of all incoming vessels arriving in a foreign port and we slipped into Baltimore Harbor by eleven-thirty.

CHAPTER 6

Collision at Sea

We sailed into the port, leaving the lighthouse on Sherkin Island to our left, and on our right a cone-shaped white tower that looked from afar like a pillar of salt. The harbor entrance was fairly narrow. Small dark caves could be seen in the rock cliffs on our starboard beam, and on the left was a large, lush island, graced with an ancient monastery.

John had mixed feelings on sighting land. Like all of us he had become accustomed to being at sea. His worries echoed those of the whole family. "Everything I had hoped would happen on the trip did. Were we now going to lose the closeness that we had developed as a family? I was excited and yet sad."

Our days in Ireland were graced by peaceful morning haze and balmy afternoons. Upon our arrival, a handsome young lad gallantly helped Elizabeth onto the quay. "The tide was out and the cement dock was high above our heads. Mom was first up the ladder. I followed. Someone grabbed my hand. I thought at first it was Mom, but suddenly I found myself lifted onto the dock. I was looking directly into the face of a complete stranger. He was adorable and he smiled. I blushed and turned to Mom. When I turned back, he was gone. Later that day, I saw him again and he and his friend invited Mom and me into the pub for a drink. His name was Jean Luc and he was wonderful. He and his friends had sailed from Belgium on a little sloop. He invited me to a dance at the yacht club that night." Elizabeth was smitten.

Al left almost immediately after our arrival. We'd been glad to have his steadfast assistance throughout the voyage, and were sad to see him go. But responsibilities in the States beckoned him home.

The people of Baltimore were homey and gracious. The little yacht club at the edge of the harbor had a dance the night of our arrival and blared American rock music, much to the delight of our kids. That first night, Cindy and I were exhausted and insisted on going back to the boat at eleven. Because we were at anchor and in a strange country, we wouldn't allow the children to stay without us. Elizabeth had fallen hard for the handsome young Belgian who had helped her off the boat. Jean Luc just as courteously escorted her onto the dance floor. We assured her that she would see him again the next day and quietly herded our flock back to the boat. We met lots of other Europeans in Baltimore Harbor. This was our first exposure to the European cruising fraternity and, although we would see few of them as we worked our way north, this loose network proved to be among our most reliable sources for friendships in the years to come. Language barriers quickly melted before the infectious gabble of our youthful crew; we were hosted at deck parties and a center of attention at the local pubs.

John met a young British lad his age and struck up a fast friendship, while Elizabeth immersed herself in a welcome social whirl. "Jean Luc and his friends took Peter and me by dinghy to climb on the rocks near the entrance to the harbor. I told them to bring their suits so we could go swimming. They said that the water was too cold, but I made fun of them and insisted that I was going. When we got there, the boys all dove in, but I refused because it *was* too cold and because there was seaweed there. They threw me in. We went back to Jean Luc's boat to taste a Belgian aperitif."

The little town boasted two pubs, each a center of warmth and hospitality. Fish and chips were the inevitable specialty of the house, and the bartenders and garrulous patrons engaged us in question and answer sessions about our voyage. In the lane that ran through the center of town stood a little grocery store where we stocked up on local farm produce. We hadn't seen fresh vegetables for about two weeks. The milk was fresh and creamy; it came in glass bottles, as I remembered it had when I was a little boy. Soft, warm light shone from the cottages lining the lane as we wound our way back to the boat at night.

The commercial quay in town was used by the fishing fleet; pleasure craft used it only for being cleared into the harbor by the customs authorities. But we were able to fill our water tanks there, replenishing the 150 gallons we had used during the crossing—rather a modest amount considering the needs of six people for three weeks. (This was helped by using saltwater to wash dishes.) Our two stern tanks, however, were contaminated with seawater. It turned out that the antisiphon loops did not work at sea, so I quickly refilled the tanks and shut off the connection of the air vents with the outside of the boat. The vents now open inside the hull, just below the deck.

Several ship's chores remained to be done those first few

days. The blocks for the twin running sail halyard had to be moved to prevent chafe. The topping lifts for the whisker poles were changed. Vents from the main and spare fuel tanks had to be separated so the spare tank could be filled. Otherwise an air lock would occur and neither tank would take fuel. The chain stripper had to be repositioned to allow the anchor windlass to work properly.

Cindy, Elizabeth, and Peter decided to take the bus to a nearby town to try and find a laundromat. Fields and farmlands lined the road, with a few cottages in between. Everywhere along the way they saw cultivated carpets of little tiny flowers clustered in bunches to look like one large one, acres of flowers, with blues blending into lavender, purple, red, yellow, orange, and white. This riot of color against the green background of field and bush was all the more arresting after our weeks at sea.

After a few days, we visited Cape Clear Island for a folk festival and subsequently motored into the harbor at Schull. The soft, green islands surrounding our anchorage looked from afar like velvet. The town of Schull lay in the lee of a low-rising hill. We rowed to the town dock with several errands on our minds. We had used up two of our four propane tanks, so Peter and I took the two tanks, heavy despite their lack of fuel, and hiked into town. When we got there, we learned that the nearest place to buy propane was in Skibbereen, a regional marketplace some fifteen miles away. We decided to try to hitch a ride. Within about ten minutes, we were lucky enough to be picked up by a thin, middle-aged man in a van. He asked where we were headed and invited us to hop in the back. He indicated that he knew two places that sold propane. Both were petrol stations. He was intrigued when we told him about our journey, and struck up an animated conversation with us. Meanwhile, he was smoking continuously and driving along this small two-lane road with trees growing right up to the edges and with no protective shoulder. There seemed barely enough room for two cars, yet we frequently encountered buses and trucks bound in the opposite direction. Our loquacious friend negotiated this tiny lane with aplomb and never decelerated. Peter and I were all the while sitting on the flat, metal floor of his van with nothing to hold onto and two large, cylindrical propane tanks that had minds of their own. We disembarked in the middle of an extremely busy small city and found a petrol station that sold propane. Then a small crisis: Our American fittings did not match European ones, and our tanks could not be filled. Friendly suggestions abounded, and we were directed to a small engineering firm to see if they could make adaptors for our fittings. We located the place and, busy as they were, the people accommodated us. With the new connectors we were able to get the tanks filled, and at last we headed back on a public bus. We arrived in Schull late that afternoon and rowed out to *Free Spirit* in a captivating sunset that set the entire town aglow in a golden warmth. We got the tanks reinstalled and I set about making dinner for the gang.

The next day, after struggling with a balky windlass that wouldn't work because of a wet relay, we finally got the anchor up and set sail along the southern coast toward Kinsale. With 900 pounds of anchor and chain securing us to the harbor bottom, the powerful electric windlass was a crucial necessity. We were hard on the wind with five-foot seas, driving to weather. The day was bright with high thin clouds rushing by in the moderately strong breeze. *Free Spirit* heeled over as she drove her stately bow into the lively seas. The crew were all in the cockpit. Cindy was resting with her eyes closed. The older two were reading. John was concentrating on a puzzle. I was below at the chart table trying to figure out an alternative harbor for the night, since we would never make Kinsale in one day. The ship had a gentle motion down below as we charged over the seas. All of a sudden there was a tremendous crash and I was thrown the full length of the cabin floor against a forward bulkhead. Struggling to my feet, I dashed to the cockpit to meet mass confusion. We had collided with a sixty-five-foot heavy wooden fishing trawler. We were still driving through the side of her beam fifteen feet forward of midship. Men in working clothes, dungarees, heavy wool sweaters, and wool stocking caps scrambled across her deck toward our foul embrace. Her planking was stove in on either side of our near fatal thrust. I scrambled for the wheel and throttled back on the power. Sails were flogging; the grinding of the two ships as they strove to master each other tore at our ears. Easing *Free Spirit* into reverse, I gently tried to extricate us from this mess. She shuddered and refused to release her hold. More power, another tearing of timber, and we were free. As we stood off and surveyed the damage, it was a sad sight. She was the *Saorise*, out of Castletown. Our starboard bow had torn a hole in the six-inch planking of her bulwark. Three feet on either side of that hole, her planking was cracked and splintered. Her owner had been paying full attention to his fishing, and our crew were facing the landward side. They never saw the *Saorise*, as she was hidden behind our yankee. We had been at a sharp angle of heel.

Poor *Free Spirit*, her sixty-pound CQR anchor was bent at right angles. The bowsprit had been literally torn off the boat and was dangling by the anchor chain. The forward chainplate was bent. The foredeck had been ripped off the hull, opening the hull-deck joint. The windlass had been torn off its mounts, taking part of the deck with it. There was a deep gouge in the gelcoat, and two feet of the teak bow rail, with the starboard chock, were gone.

We limped into Baltimore Harbor. The kids were totally silent in their shock. Cindy and I never even looked at each other. It was too painful. How ironic this was. We had crossed the Atlantic without incident, and now, while cruising the coast, we had gotten into trouble. For three weeks we had kept twenty-four-hour watches through fair weather and foul. Now, in bright sunshine, and with perfect visibility, we had let our guard down for about fifteen minutes. How awful to have our adventure end this way. Norway was now an impossible dream. We would have to spend the rest of the summer getting repairs done.

The yard in Baltimore Harbor was unable to assist with repairs; they only dealt in steel and wood, not fiberglass. The nearest place for repairs would be Cork and that was a hundred miles to windward. With an open foredeck, this seemed like a foolhardy option.

When placed in such a predicament, you have two choices: lie down and accept one's fate, or inwardly scream *no* and decide to change it. I decided to do the repairs myself. With only hand tools—a hacksaw, hand drill, screwdriver, wrenches, hammer, and vise grips—I set out to accomplish the impossible. As I inspected the damage, I realized how fortunate we were to have had a boat constructed as solidly as *Free Spirit*. Despite the massive impact to her bow, there was no damage to the hull itself. It was entirely intact. Another less sturdy boat involved in such a collision would have had its bow torn off completely and gone to the bottom. We had a collision bulkhead for just such a catastrophe, but it was not needed.

Not only did the deck have to be sealed, but I would have to replace the bowsprit and windlass, to handle our anchors. The twisted CQR anchor could be replaced with the seventy-five-pound kedge I kept in the bilge. I made a large backing plate from some spare 1/4-inch aluminum stock I had aboard. This I cut with a hacksaw to fit the foredeck. The fragments of deck left were strong enough to act as an anchor for the plate. The yard was able to sell me some large bolts and I then bolted the bowsprit and windlass back down to the plate. All was then sealed with underwater epoxy. I worked all through that night and into the next evening and, by midnight the second day, the repairs were completed.

We were visited the following day by a surveyor representing the *Saorise*'s insurance company. He went over the details of the accident and examined my repairs. I asked him if *Free Spirit* looked safe enough to go to sea. He told me that if he owned a boatyard he would hire me in a minute, and he pronounced the repairs seaworthy!

We hung the big Herreshoff kedge off the end of the newly positioned bowsprit, tied one of the flukes at the rail, and set off again on our cruise. We stopped into Castletown and then Glengariff, both in Bantry Bay. The latter was a bustling, modern little town with more local wealth than other places we had been. Elaborately landscaped gardens graced several of the estates there. In Glengariff, we stopped at an ice cream shop for banana splits, much more modest than the exotic concoctions in the States, and spent a delightful day as tourists. We peeked into every shop we could find. In the harbor a small island owned by a British earl had been stocked with exotic plants from around the world. We anchored next to the boat belonging to the prime minister of the Irish Republic. Unfortunately, he was not aboard while we were there, but we did at least get to see his boat.

Stopping in Adrigole on the way, we then cruised up the Kenmare River. We anchored at midnight in the entrance to Sneem. The next day we were invited to attend what turned out to be a local talent night. Anyone who wished could stand up and tell a joke or sing a song. Since everyone knew that we were from the American boat that had sailed from the States, we were asked if we would like to join in. I am the only ham in the family, so I got up and sang a ballad, for which I was roundly cheered. We all had a great time and got in after midnight. The following day, we took our leave past the forbidding Bull Rock at the mouth of the Kenmare River.

"As we left Ireland, I put on the tape deck. I played, 'Open Arms' by Journey. It was a love song and I played it in memory of Jean Luc and it made me cry."—Elizabeth

"I felt nervous about heading to sea again."—Peter

"I could feel the growth in my seamanship and had developed my sea legs. I had more confidence in myself. When we got to Norway, I was able to help with docking and cleating down the lines for the first time."—John

"We were now on our own, just the family, and I liked that."—Cindy

CHAPTER 7

Arctic Adventure

Misted over in memory are sunlit scenes of bundled-up children, arms lifted in joy as they slide down a snow-covered slope. They fall over each other, laughing and smiling, seemingly beckoning to all children everywhere to join them as they slide. Such are the vestiges of my early recollections of childhood picture books from the land of the midnight sun. Full-bearded adventures in leather togs fiercely led their Viking ships from clefts in the mountains on voyages of exploration and conquest.

What was that world like? Is it still there? How could one cross the great ocean and not find out? In planning our journey, as a pragmatic matter, I had to consider the realities of wind direction, ocean currents, and cruising seasons. The powerful easterly winds sweep across the Atlantic to the British Isles and beyond. The prevailing winds along the European coast blow north to south. It became obvious that if we wished to visit northern Europe, we should start there and work our way south, eventually crossing back to America via the southeast trades.

In order to gain some insight into the projected passage,

I read widely about Scandinavian history, weather, geology, and folklore. Formed by the glaciers of the Pleistocene period some two million years past, the deep oceanic inlets called fjords finger their way through mountain passes up to 115 miles inland. Peopled by hunters and fisherman as long as eight to ten thousand years ago, Norway also has large burial grounds dating to the more recent Bronze Age presenting evidence of early social organization. From the early part of the Christian era until A.D. 800 to 900, Norway was populated by several small kingdoms formed by nomadic Germanic tribes. On June 8, A.D. 793, Viking raiders sacked the small tidal island of Lindisfarne off Britain's east coast and initiated a 250-year era of bloody raids, exploration, colonization, and far-flung trade by a dynamic, vital, and rough-hewn people. Spawned by a feudal system whereby the firstborn son inherited the family holdings while later offspring tried to occupy and preempt distant lands, the Viking raiders sailed from these very same fjords.

Warming weather trends during the eighth century increased crop growth and population in Scandinavian countries. Since the right of primogeniture prevailed, when all usable land was taken, a suitable occupation had to be found for younger sons. It was also part of the tradition that a young man could not marry until he was able to provide his wife with a home and hearth. Wealthy older men could afford several young wives to warm up their declining years, but the young men were eventually compelled to seek foreign wives and foreign homes.

Iceland was settled by these young Vikings; they discovered and briefly inhabited the North American continent; they conquered Ireland. These determined wanderers and conquerors influenced the entire character of England and the rest of southern Europe. This was a recorded migration, probably similar to population movements that have punctuated earth's history for thousands of years. Christianity modified the Norsemen and eliminated polygamy. Married into foreign cultures, their sons gradually assimilated into those cultures, leaving Norse names for current cities and towns and Scandinavian features on the faces of the children. In Ireland, Limerick was once Hlymnekr, Wexford was Veigsfjörth, and Wicklow was Vikingslo.

With this exciting and romantic history as a background, it seemed natural to plan our adventure with Norway as a primary goal. We would chance the same drama and risk of exploration as that undertaken by the Norsemen of old. I was determined to find and explore those lore-laden fjords, for they vibrated with the living history of a great people.

Stretching 1600 miles from well above the arctic circle to the Skagerrak facing Denmark, Norway's coast is bathed by the Gulf Stream, which moderates her weather and prevents some of the extremes that her northern latitudes would otherwise dictate. (Inland up north is another story, and temperatures below minus forty degrees are not uncommon in winter.) Sognafjord, Geirangerfjord, Romsdalsfjord, Hardangerfjord—Viking lairs of the past, canyons of adventure and exploration for the present. Many people today in this Norwegian outback live simple lives dependent on fishing and farming.

We set our course to the northwest to gain some offing. Years spent around boats teach one that the greatest dangers to a ship are found near shore. Only there do adverse currents drive one onto a hidden shoal. Near the coast one's helm must be attended constantly. Better to run out to sea. Eighty miles off the Irish coast we turned north to head for the far northern reaches of the Atlantic and the entrance to the North Sea. Our shakedown as a boat and crew were behind us; now we were entirely on our own.

All medications for seasickness control available to us in the States had proved useless. We had started with Transderm (scopolamine) patches behind the ears. They didn't work and gave both Cindy and Elizabeth blurred vision. A concoction suggested by a pharmacist in Nantucket using Phenergan and ephedrine proved similarly worthless. Dramamine had failed us on prior trips, and even injectable Compazine wasn't able to help Wayne on our abortive first start. In Baltimore Harbor, however, we first learned of Stügeron (cinnarizine 15 mg). Manufactured and sold by Janssen Pharmaceutical in England, it is an antihistamine marketed throughout Europe for motion sickness. Our Belgian and French friends swore by it. We bought some in Skibbereen and started it twelve hours prior to starting the next long leg of our cruise. For 1100 miles we sailed up the west coast of Ireland and across the heaving North Sea and none of us became ill. It was like a miracle.

Two days out we helped John celebrate his eleventh birthday. It was a most fair and lovely day. The wind veered around, allowing us to lay our course northward at about six knots. I made John potato pancakes at his request, and a big vanilla birthday cake. You can't buy presents at sea, so we each gave John something special: an eleven-minute backrub, an offer to serve his watch, a promissory note to take his turn at the dishes, and so on. Despite the lack of packaged presents, I think that John appreciated the personal kind even more. He did note that the cake had a list to it similar to the heel of the boat, in spite of the use of a gimballed (free-swinging) oven.

We motorsailed all that night because the wind was light and on our nose. The most striking difference we noted between this trip and our transatlantic crossing was that we were no longer afraid. It was a subtle thing, and one we wouldn't have admitted earlier. Cindy and the kids were more relaxed, and the "scupper" no longer took everything so seriously either. We found that we got into a sea routine more easily and adapted to conditions more quickly.

Routine rather than rotating watches worked better for us. On many boats, watches are rotated so that no one feels stuck with the worst duty. Our watches were chosen with individual personal characteristics in mind. Peter could not stay up past midnight. He would fall asleep on his feet if he did. Elizabeth and Cindy are night people. Elizabeth therefore took the midnight to 2:00 A.M. watches, Cindy did the 2:00 to 4:00 A.M. stint, and I was on from 4:00 to 6:00 A.M. Daytime shifts were longer. I would prepare breakfast when I got off watch, wake John, and begin taking sights around 9:00 A.M. After plotting our estimated position, I went to bed. Peter took over at 9:00 A.M. from John and the rotations continued from there. The family no longer had to wake me up for sail changes and similar chores in the middle of the night, so I was more rested.

The northeast North Atlantic was actually beautiful that third night at sea. The sun had set but the sky was still a deep blue at 10:30 P.M. in all directions except near the horizon toward the north. Notes from my log read: "A low line of gray clouds with no substance to them lies to the west. No other clouds are visible on the horizon. The seas are lively but have no weight to them. They lightly lift us on their shoulders and carry us forward for awhile, then gently leave us to seek other sport. We are running under a beam to broad reach under the twin wings with the mainsail up to ease the roll." (As the ship rolls to one side, the strapped-in mainsail catches the wind and cushions the roll, dampening the extremity of movement that otherwise would occur.) "A two-thirds moon has risen high in the east and we haven't seen a ship since leaving the Kenmare river. It is very peaceful knowing that we are truly alone and that there are no shipping lanes nearby. I contrast this with my panic in mid-Atlantic when I first realized how alone we could be at sea."

July twenty-ninth dawned gray and cloudy. At sea more than most other places one's moods can be much affected by the weather. It was cool and winds were moderate from our quarter at about fifteen to twenty knots. We cleared the Hebrides without actually seeing them. We'd gone 450 miles and had another 650 or so to go. The ship rolled and pitched over the twelve-foot seas. Norway beckoned, but on that day I wondered in my log whether even that prospect was worth the penalty of these many days at sea. I enjoy coastal sailing and gunkholing. Even the occasional overnight jaunt is all right with me, but days and days or perhaps weeks at sea I find too debilitating. "Now this is more like the gray, cold, overcast, windswept north Atlantic that I've come to know and dislike," I wrote in my log. "Her irresistible embrace seems to sweep all within her clutches into the cavernous wasteland of her bosom. Not one to pick favorites, she takes one and all on a whirlwind ride, sending them skittering first to one side and then the other. Her single most malignant characteristic is her unpredictability. She will send you five or nine or thirty-two easy rolling waves to lull you into a sense of confidence. She then raps you hard with a big roller, sending your ship skittering on the edges of control and you sideways in midstep from your purchase on the companionway ladder. The resultant bruises and four-letter words add to the general desolation of the scene. She is happy. We are not. The endless reaches of gray-flecked foam seem to rear back and taunt us with their insensitivity.

"Slowly, ever so slowly, our barometer seems to be stopping its slide down the millibars. Today is a day to concentrate on writing and reading. We are keeping ten-minute watches by the kitchen timer. That means that we leave the warmth of our cabin for the bitter cold of the North Sea air to check our horizon every ten minutes. Cindy was on at 5:00 P.M. and lo and behold, we almost ran into another fishing boat. This Norwegian trawler veered out of our way. It seemed that a fine haze had come on so subtly that we had not realized that the limits of our vision had been so drastically curtailed. Cindy had actually gone up two minutes early and was shocked to see the near collision. We started up our radar and cut the time of our visual watches to five minutes. At this point we were ninety miles north of the Hebrides."

There is no question that the most dangerous aspect of ocean sailing is other shipping. It is not possible with a small crew on a long voyage to keep someone on deck twenty-four hours a day for days or weeks at a time. This is even more true here in the high latitudes. It's just too bone-chilling cold!

We were under engine power at the same latitude as Iceland—about a thousand miles north of Boston. Our expected time of arrival in Trondheim: August third. I played Scrabble with Elizabeth then hearts with all three kids. We listened to a Sherlock Holmes adventure on the BBC and soon it was my watch again. Here in the wasteland of the North Atlantic we spent some memorable evenings. I had recorded some taped adventure and mystery stories from our library. I intended them for John, but after dinner, while Cindy cleaned up the dishes, the three kids and I would curl up on the bunk in the "library" and listen to these stories. We all shared in the excitement and wonder of adventures much as did my own generation before the advent of television. Somehow, the painting of stories with words is more powerful and allows us to share the experience. When your attention is riveted to the TV, you screen out those around you. Radio can be shared. TV is a lonely pursuit.

We motored throughout the night and morning. Directly between the Faeroe and Shetland Island groups, with clear skies, sunshine, and light fog with no wind, we saw a pod of blue whales. Rising together, their mammoth forms gracefully arched through the water two hundred yards off our beam. Their blow was clearly audible as well as visible, and they moved like gigantic, slow-moving, playful dolphins. As we closed under engine power for some photos, one of the leviathans, half again as long as *Free Spirit*, rose and plunged under the water, leaving a hole about thirty feet in diameter and ten feet deep next to our rail.

The wind increased on our nose all night, gradually slowing our speed under engine and a sheeted mainsail from 3 to 1.5 knots. Driven farther and farther south of our course, we soon realized that we couldn't raise Trondheim in those conditions. We turned north to try to work our way nearer land. Again, the driving wind and steep twelve-foot seas prevented us from laying a course toward the coast. It seemed, however, that the northern course drew us closer to our goal than its sister, so I decided to continue in this direction. We were now on a latitude due west of Trondheim. I guessed that if we could hold our course another day, we would be able to fall off for our destination.

The day stayed grim and bleak, despite breaks of sun through the clouds. Gray-crested monsters with black bellies tore out of the Arctic gloom at our ship. *Free Spirit* shuddered as she struck each rolling colossus. The battle was fierce. Cindy stood beside me, transfixed by the scene. The kids stayed below out of the frigid air. The busy and tireless engine gave the cabin a little warmth as long as we kept the doors to the engine compartment open, but its deep-throated rumbling prevented sleep.

Although no one was seasick, the constant motion was exhausting. At midnight, we were still driving along. The sun still showed part of her fiery curve as we peaked each towering crest. Our breath hung crystalline in the air and the dark clouds overhead reflected the sun's wan glow. As we dropped into each valley, the world became dark again.

Finally, as morning approached and the sun started to be visible even in the wave valleys, the wind's strength began to falter and we headed south again on a course that could just reach the outer Trondheimfjord, the first landfall we'd planned for Norway. Cindy and I went to bed, leaving Peter on watch. We drove on through the day and again into the bright night. No longer could we tell the difference between the two except, perhaps, by degree. We had reached a latitude equal to the northern reaches of Iceland and now were ready to lay our course to Trondheim.

Norway, however, had other plans for us. She sent another cold blast at us that day from a direction that caused us to veer off again southward. Once more we were driven far from our course. We tacked, and headed north. As the wind strength increased to gale force, we were repeatedly forced to reduce our sail area until we had nothing up but a reefed yankee. As we drove through the northern reaches of the North Sea, we began to keep our eyes peeled for the oil rigs that dot these waters. That day remained a hard one. We rolled along into the wind, tacking one way and then the other.

It was so frustrating. The wind kept coming from the northeast, preventing us from making any but slow progress toward Trondheim. We were pounding in the bigger seas so badly that Peter and I shifted 200 feet of ⅜-inch chain from the anchor locker back to the shower room. A lot of weight is carried forward, with our 140-pound dinghy on the foredeck, 120 pounds of anchors, and 800 pounds of chain. The entire boat shook. There's nothing like a hard beat to weather to clarify problems aboard a yacht. With the chain drawn further aft, the pounding lessened and we drove on.

August second, 7:46 P.M.: I made a devil of a picture. Bundled up in an undershirt, long underwear top and bottom, flannel shirt, wool sweater, foul-weather jacket, dungarees, socks and wool mittens on my feet. And those feet were stuck into the engine room compartment for heat. Beef stroganoff and rice for lunch and dinner barely relieved the gloom.

Again, I'm preoccupied by the question of why I subject all of us to this insanity. Maybe because there is something maddeningly boring about life in the twentieth century. We live in comfort; there's little to tax our spirit. Life is so safe, so sure, so damn easy. The human spirit needs challenge and danger to be uplifted. It needs horizons to conquer. And so there is satisfaction in testing oneself, meeting the sea on its own terms and taking everything it can give. With a smile on my face, I slowly drifted off to sleep.

We had touched on the arctic circle, up at the high latitudes where the sun never set. I had expected icebergs and polar bears and snow-capped glaciers, but all we saw were endless reaches of ocean and the march of Neptune's mindless minions sweeping down from the Arctic.

The next day was cold, crisp, and clear. We had lots of sunshine and twenty knots of wind directly out of the northeast. We tacked to a position about 20 miles north and 100 miles west of Trondheim and at that point we fell off on a course for Kristiansund. In order to make Trondheim, the ancient Viking capital, we would have had to sail north and south, one tack and then the other, for at least two more days, gradually working our way to windward. An end run into Kristiansund would satisfy our desire to see the northern fjords even if we had to sacrifice exploring Trondheim. At that point I knew little of the character of Norwegian communities like Kristiansund, and I had only read of Trondheim in some of the old histories. We really wanted to see the fjords. Little did we realize what special treats awaited us in those unknown Norwegian towns. We slipped over onto a southeast tack and set our course for Kristiansund. We hoped to arrive at the offshore islands at two or three in the morning.

CHAPTER 8

Kristiansund

Arise, arise, oh my fair crew
For what have we now here
A vast enchanting hazy view
Of Norway's outer sphere.

We worked our way into Kristiansund on the morning of August 4, 1982. We had made the trip from Boston to Norway, with all our trials, the failed initial start, and the sojourn in Ireland, in a total of eight weeks. Others, of course, had come our way before. Most had made the trip the other way.

On October 15, 1825, the New York *Advertiser* featured a front-page article entitled "A Novel Sight," which contained the following passage: "A vessel has arrived at this port, with emigrants, from Norway. The vessel is very small—forty-five American tons—and brought forty-six passengers, male and female, all bound to Ontario county in western New York state. . . . The appearance of such a party of strangers, coming from so distant a country, and in a vessel of a size apparently ill-calculated for a voyage across the Atlantic, could not but excite an unusual degree of interest." The newspaper said the trip had taken fourteen weeks and that the ship was a single-masted fishing boat from the town of Stavanger. One child was born on the way. (At least that was one bit of excitement denied to us.)

To understand Norway it is useful to go back in time to the Middle Ages, when Norway's grip on the western world began to slip. Her sons and daughters had been assimilated into the cultures of their adopted countries. Long, cold winters reasserted themselves, limiting energy and resources for population growth and exploration. In the fourteenth century, the Black Plague decimated the country and reduced her population to a few thousand. Undermanned and weakened, Norway was no longer a match for Sweden and Denmark. Swedish and Danish kings ruled her in succession and she lost her long-cherished independence.

In 1814, Denmark, which had sided with France during the Napoleonic wars, was forced to give up the land of Norway. In the Treaty of Kiel, Norway was ceded to Sweden. A storm of anger swept the country. The popular Danish royal governor called for a constitutional assembly. Small landowners—many of them subsistence farmers and merchants—were tired of being overtaxed by the corrupt government and overtithed by an equally corrupt church. The assembly convened at Eidsvoll, forty miles north of Oslo, and adopted a democratic, liberal constitution with some of the same features as the brand new, much-admired American constitution.

Although Norway declared her independence, she was unable to enforce this declaration militarily. But after some negotiation with Sweden, she retained the right to rule her own internal affairs while still flying the Swedish flag. On the seventeenth of May, 1814, independence was claimed.

The date is still celebrated as Norway's Independence Day (Syttende Mai). It wasn't until 1905 that the union of Norway with Sweden was peacefully ended. Though relations with Sweden had been tense, the Danes had been protectors of the Norweigans in years gone by. Thus a Danish prince was elected to the throne.

The nineteenth century saw a dramatic flourishing of Norwegian arts and a resurgence of its culture. Ivar Aasen rekindled interest in and acceptance of the Norwegian language, spoken at that time only in the remote villages and valleys. Traveling far and wide, he collected all the significant words of the people and wrote a grammar and dictionary of their language, called *landsmaal*. Those who still looked to Denmark as the source of culture opposed this movement, but pride in the homeland helped it spread.

In music, Edvard Grieg gave the world romantic melodies extolling the beauties of the northern mountains. (We kept tapes of his *Peer Gynt Suite* and *Norwegian Melodies* on hand for frequent use at sea and in the fjords. He was an old favorite of mine.)

While all this was occurring, many anachronisms from the feudal age still weighed heavily on Norwegian society. From the eleventh century onward, a gradually increasing number of military and state officials and a multitude of clergy dominated the country with misrule, extortion, and waste. The substitution of Lutheran precepts for Roman Catholicism made little difference as far as the exploitation of the rural class was concerned. The church operated under the principle of charging what the market would bear. For a people struggling with the soil to make a bare subsistence, otherworldliness appealed and they were devout Lutherans.

In the meantime, the *bønder* (small landowners) were

being ignored by the aristocracy in the Storting (parliament). Giving lip service to egalitarian ideals, they maintained laws permitting those with money to hire substitutes for military service. The burden of such service naturally fell disproportionately upon the poor.

High taxes on land forced many farmers to sell part of their holdings to lighten their tax burden. This breakup of the land into thousands of holdings of less than ten acres each meant that insufficient food to support a family could be produced on each homestead. After a succession of crop failures in the 1830s, the population of entire valleys emigrated to the United States. By going to America, or to the growing cities of Norway, they hoped to avoid starvation.

Letters from friends and relatives who had emigrated, and visiting emigres dressed in fine clothes like the aristocracy, caused a storm of interest in America to sweep across the land. Today it is hard to find a Norwegian who does not have a relative living in the States. These immigrants took with them deeply rooted customs and beliefs and enriched the American cultural scene. With the seemingly unlimited opportunities available to them, 754,561 people emigrated between 1825 and 1915—this from a country whose population in 1825 was only 1,035,345. America gave these people better security and social position and a system of laws not unlike their own, but to the end of his days the Norwegian-American harbored a longing for the sight of his home fjord glittering in the sun and the sound of the roaring waterfall hard by the cottage where he had been born.

The 1600-mile Norwegian west coast extends from its southern view of Denmark and the Skagerrak to the chilly reaches of the Arctic Ocean and the Barents Sea. It is a long, thin nation, in some places barely 100 miles wide. A spine of mountains guards the western coast from north to south, while in the southeast, plains touch gently on Sweden. Norway shares a long border with Sweden; its northern plateaus are shared with Finland; its very northernmost tip nestles uncomfortably against the Soviet Union.

We made our landfall at Kristiansund, about 150 miles south of the arctic circle, hoving to off the coast at 2:00 A.M. in the soft glow of the arctic summer night. The sun, just below the horizon, still gave off enough illumination to highlight the mountains. The sky was a light blue gray, with mountains and islets black in relief. The water reflected the light from the sky. Surrounded by thousands of islets and rocks, we drifted quietly in the dying breeze.

We had a running fix from a satellite reading eight hours earlier, and we knew our position within about ten miles, but there were no buoys or other distinguishing marks along the coast save for lighthouses casting their beacons on an otherwise primordial scene. Spotted every ten miles or so along the coast, these sentinels had none of the individualized light characteristics found in New England waters. Each one had its own red, white, and green segments indicating unsafe and safe passages, but no distinctive features or coded flash to mark its identity. From our vantage point ten miles to seaward, there was nothing but solid mountain rock and cliffs to our lee. We would have to wait until later in the morning, when I could take a sun line to define our position more accurately.

Around five in the morning we spotted a line of fishing boats exiting from a mountain cleft and we headed toward the lead boat under power at top speed. We flagged down one of the boats and called out, "Kristiansund, Kristiansund, where is Kristiansund?" Indecipherable mutterings were the captain's response. I held up a chart and pointed to it, again yelling, "Kristiansuuund?" After this exercise had been repeated four or five times, the light seemed to dawn. "Ah, Kreestiansoond—da. Da." He pointed toward a particularly high mountain. I waved a thank-you and pointed our bow toward the solid rock. Keeping a close watch for rocks in the otherwise deep waters, we skirted a few islets and motored toward the solid wall of the mountains. At last, after long anxious moments, the mountainous wall parted and we were in an outer fjord off the coast of Norway.

The western coast of Norway is a triumph of protective topography. Beyond the series of alpine ranges split by deep, wide fjords striking deep into the heart of the country lies a barrier of mountainous offshore islands. These create a seawall that guards the coast from the ravages of the North Sea. Between these islands and the mountains of the coast is a long, broad waterway that traverses the entire length of the country from well above the arctic circle to well below Bergen, the major coastal seaport. Seaward of the islands lies a ten-mile stretch of islets and rocks, which look on a chart as if a painter has taken his brush and carelessly spattered the canvas.

We motored into the little harbor of Kristiansund at 8:00 A.M. Tall, painted, peak-roofed houses lined the harbor. Old warehouses vied with commercial fishing vessels and cargo ships for dock space. We tied up to the town quay and promptly fell asleep. At eleven that morning, Elizabeth awoke with a start and called to me. Sleeping in a bunk next to the open companionway, she had looked out to see perhaps a hundred townspeople on the quay, standing and staring at our boat with its sleeping crew. I arose and waved hello, and we soon found ourselves the center of the town's attention. People buzzed all about us as we tried to explain who we were and how we had arrived there. Some spoke English; many didn't. A young woman reporter from the local newspaper appeared, took our picture, and sat with Cindy in the cockpit for an hour, drinking in our adventure. (The paper published the picture and our story the next day.) Peter and I headed for the local police station to find out how to clear through customs. This was a formality that was always required but seldom made difficult in our travels. Here we ran into a slight problem: Norwegian law allowed us to keep the boat in Norway for a maximum of six months, but we needed to have the damage acquired in Ireland repaired, and that would necessitate leaving *Free Spirit* over the winter. We applied for special permission to leave her for up to a year. To help us in our quest, I cabled Eric and Kari, a young couple from Oslo whom we had met when I gave a talk at a Norwegian–American Club at home. Eric's father had some influence and could, perhaps, help us. We were told that it would be weeks, perhaps months, before an answer would be forthcoming.

Apparently it was quite unusual for a sailboat to visit this part of the world, especially one with an American flag on her transom. When we got back to the boat after our customs visit, we found that several people were still standing and staring at our boat. A few offered advice about places to visit in the vicinity, and one gentleman went off and returned with a group of charts of the local waters.

Having cleared customs, we worked on a myriad of jobs. The outboard motor had packed up in Ireland and had to be taken in for repairs. The relay for the windlass needed to be replaced. I repaired three seams that had opened up in the yankee in the last gale, and filled the boat with fuel and water.

A well-dressed, trim, blond man in slacks and an open-necked short-sleeved shirt introduced himself. John, who owned a very large department store complex, drove Peter, Elizabeth, and the outboard in his car to a repair place. He and his wife, Solveig, offered us the use of their washer and dryer at home, lent us a car, and asked us over to visit. Chris, the owner of another major department store, went over our charts with us, offered to fill in details of the Geirangerfjord, a popular and especially scenic thrust of the sea into Norway's heartland, and pointed out several good spots to visit. Kaaby, an electrical engineer, offered to repair our windlass and then wouldn't charge us for the two hours' time he spent reinstalling the new relay. The outboard motor repair shop, at our new friend John's suggestion, refused to take any money for fixing our outboard. A former sea captain named Nils bought us a loran chart of western Norway and wouldn't accept payment for it. He also gave us the name of his son-in-law in Molde in case we should visit.

Odd, a former captain in the merchant marine, took us by car all around Kristiansund. A member of a local cruising club that also counted many of the other notables in town among its members, he showed us a Kristiansund from days of old as well as the present. Kristiansund is a modern, airy, and pleasant little city sitting on an island with a background of mountains. When visiting Europe, it is impossible not to be reminded at some point of the tragedy of World War II. Here in Kristiansund, it inflicted terrible scars. The city was entirely destroyed by the Germans during the war. As Odd pointed proudly to all the beautiful buildings and homes, he remarked sadly that the old city had also been beautiful in its own way.

When war broke out in Europe in 1939, the majority of Norwegians could not believe that Germany would ever attack them. It was unthinkable. All Norway desired was to live in peace. They had no quarrel with the German people, no shared borders—why fear attack? Consequently, when they were suddenly invaded, they were taken completely by surprise and were confused and astonished.

The attack took place on April 9, 1940, and involved the simultaneous invasion of Oslo, Kristiansand, Stavanger, Bergen, Trondheim, and Narvik. Airborne troops were landed at the airport in Oslo and after a short, fierce firefight with the Norwegian Royal Guards, marched triumphantly down the main street in Oslo to the stupefaction of the local citizens. Subterfuge, foggy weather, lack of preparation by the defenders, and an act of treason by the local commander in Narvik allowed the completion of the invasion within a few hours.

Systematic brutality by the new, illegal government, the wholesale plunder of the Norwegian treasury, food and materiel shortages, and severe inflation began to wear on the people, but despite desecration of their traditions of freedom and respect for the law, they never gave in to the oppressors. Increasing defiance of the Germans—a courageous resistance movement, sabotage, underground newspapers and radio, and insults in the press—hardened their determination to remain loyal to the legal government and the exiled king. "Never here," the Norwegian outlook common before World War II, has been replaced with "never again." Hence Norway's participation in NATO and their current defense system.

The new church in Kristiansund is symbolic of the city's revival. It is a beautiful modern structure with exquisite stained glass windows and a magnificent pipe organ. Located on top of a hill, it is approached by a series of steps with terraced flower gardens on either side. The church's jutting shape matches the jagged peaks of the mountains that surround the town.

That night we were invited to dinner at John and Solveig's lovely home on a private little harbor on the opposite side of the island from the town. His entire family was there to greet us, including his children and their grandparents. We had a delicious meal with this gracious family and slept peacefully on our boat in their harbor that night.

We received an invitation from Chris and his wife Aileen to join them the next day for a cruise with three other boats for a dinner in Aure. We took John and Solveig's daughters, fourteen-year-old Cecilie and ten-year-old Jannecke with us for our rendezvous with Chris and his friends. That night, Chris took us to a delightful hotel on the water for dinner. Odd, our host on the tour of Kristiansund and one of the members of the sailing club, made a long, polished toast to us and I returned one to all our hosts. It was a relaxing, beautiful evening with good food, good friends, some dancing, and song. The next day we planned lunch with other members of the club.

Peter and Cecilie, a pretty young lady with sandy-colored hair, startling blue eyes, and occasional freckles on her seamless young face, began to demonstrate mutual attraction as we set sail for our first cruise down the fjords.

Before Cindy or I knew what was happening, they were holding hands and quietly talking on the foredeck. Cecilie was generally quiet and retiring, but Janneke was quite a little devil, who always spoke her mind and seemed quite self-assured. Both girls belonged to a children's choir at school. As we traveled down the waterways over the next two days, they taught us the harmonies to their Norwegian folk melodies, and since this is something Cindy and I have enjoyed doing together ever since we were in school, we soon learned them well. Although we listened carefully to the pronunciation of the strange Norwegian words, it was a slow syllable-by-syllable process to mastery. Eventually, we were all singing the songs lustily as we motored down the otherwise silent fjord.

The fjords here are bordered by low, green hills with mountains in the background. Trees are plentiful and farm crops are laid out in neat rows. As we traveled back to Kristiansund to drop off Cecilie and Janneke, we had to decide whether to sail south of the island upon which Kristiansund stands or save four hours by taking the shorter northern route. The problem was a bridge with a height of twenty meters spanning the northern entrance to the harbor. (The southern entrance is open.) Looking up at our mast, I wasn't exactly sure of our height in feet, never mind meters. All I could remember at that point was that there are 2.54 centimeters to an inch. That works out to thirty-nine inches to a meter, or sixty-five feet of clearance under the bridge. I figured that our mast, which I knew to be sixty-five feet long, measured about sixty-four feet or so from the waterline of the boat since it is stepped on the keel. Should we try it? It would save us close to four hours. Yes, but let's do it carefully. How? Elizabeth loves a trip up the mast! To her, being hauled up on a halyard in a bosun's chair is fun. To me, it borders on terror. I'm deathly afraid of heights. Well, it was up the mast in the chair for Elizabeth as we approached the bridge. Closer, closer, back her down. "Dad, I'm not sure." Closer. "I think it'll be okay." "Wait, go back." And we're through. Elizabeth closed her eyes at the last minute and we scraped our VHF antenna on the bridge's underside.

Back in Kristiansund, the five kids went out to stretch their legs, and returned with a huge bag of freshly boiled shrimp. They had purchased them from an immaculate pushcart, one of many filling the quayside every day at an open fish market. Cecilie's expert fingers flew as she peeled every shrimp in the bag while we stared in amazement. Five minutes later, we sat contentedly munching on shrimp in cocktail sauce as the sun gradually dropped down over the still, picturesque harbor.

The next day we were invited to dinner with Lolo, owner of a large fish export business, and his wife Karin. They fed us freshly smoked salmon. Lolo was fascinated with our voyage and expressed an interest in joining us the following year when we planned to sail from Norway to England. Apparently there are others with a hunger for adventure. Lolo and Karin mentioned friends in Bergen who, they believed, would know the boatyard situation there and might be able to help us get repairs to our bow done. I carefully noted down names and addresses.

In the meantime, our energetic youngsters were making their own friends. John invited three boys to sleep on board one night and two arrived with wonderful presents. One brought a picture he had laboriously drawn of our boat. Another gave us a silver spoon with an ornate emblem and the name Kristiansund embossed in red and gold on the handle. John told us how he met his new friends: "I got up on the dock and saw these kids on their bikes looking at the boat. I started talking with them and they were really friendly. One of them invited me to his house and they took me to a movie—it wasn't in English. We went bike-riding around town and played soccer. I couldn't believe they accepted me as if I'd always lived there. They spoke English, which they learned in school, but slowly. We buzzed around in the dinghy and jumped the big boats' wakes. It was great to be around kids my own age."

Finally, it was time for us to leave. We shared sweet and tender good-byes with all our newfound friends. Perhaps a dozen people stood on the headland to wave as we cleared the harbor and raised sail. Sweet and tender good-byes to you, Kristiansund. We love you all.

Norwegian folk song celebrating the coming of spring*

TRANSLATION

> *All the birds have returned.*
> *Four different ones sing each day.*
> *Others sing while soaring cross the sky.*
> *They call the Spring to come once again.*
> *They implore ice and snow to go once again.*
> *Here it shall be all sun and happiness.*

*One of the songs taught to us by Cecilie and Janneke as we cruised down the fjords.

Al - le fug-ler sma de _ er ko -mmet nu til - ba-kr.

Gjek og si -sik trost og - star, Syn -ger al -le da -ge

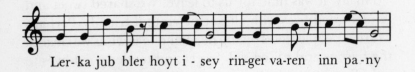

Ler-ka jub bler hoyt i - sey rin-ger va-ren inn pa -ny

Frost og sne de ma -tte_ fly Her er sol og gle-de.

CHAPTER 9

Escape from Disaster

We stayed in the vicinity of that warm and inviting community for approximately six days, and then decided to move down the coast and explore the wild and wonderful fjords of Norway. We made our way in sunshine out toward the outer fjord, a north-south waterway. Unfortunately, about ten miles south of our position there was a bridge in the fjord that was too low for our sixty-four-foot mast to pass beneath. Bridge heights were clearly marked on the charts, and there was no way to avoid this one unless we had a lower mast, so we were forced to travel the next thirty miles or so outside the protecting islands before we could duck in for our next stop at Ålesund. Many of the most dramatic fjords of the coast were south of us. Names like Geirangerfjord and Sognafjord had been bandied about by our Kristiansund friends as places we had to visit.

The decision to sail within the north-south waterway comes from the characteristics of the North Sea. It is shallow and quickly develops high steep seas in the prevalent gale force conditions. Additionally, the waters near the coast are peppered with innumerable rocks and islets that require careful navigation. It was preferable to wend our way within the waterway and its connecting fjords and their more sheltered waters. This seemed to us the only safe way to sail that area unless one was going to cross to Scotland. (When we actually made that trip the following year, it was so difficult that I almost gave up on sailing.) Not all fjords run east-west into the mountains; many run north-south and are simply narrow waterways between mountainous islands. The north-south channel we often cruised is considered a fjord in Norwegian terminology. Even the little fjords with their many small spars, rocks, and bridges are not difficult to use. The bridge heights are indicated on charts, and the narrows are well marked with perches (sticks in the water with a wooden arrow on top indicating the preferred channel) and spars.

The weather in the fjord country can be beautiful or absolutely wild. Changes occur quickly and the pleasant coolness of a sunny day can turn quickly to raw, bitter cold. After all, we were a thousand miles north of Boston. The winds tended to blow hard much of the time, but bad-weather winds always struck from the south and sunny-weather winds came from the north.

We slipped out of the north-south waterway between two of the protecting islands and followed a course toward the open sea. Before us stretched a broad bay ringed with unmarked rocks and unnamed islets. Beyond this bay lay a natural line of rocks and islets with a parallel line of rocks to seaward of these. These created a passage south. As we traversed the half-mile-wide, ten-mile-long ribbon of water, we found ourselves about five miles off the coastal islands. We headed south under power toward a natural breakwater with a small pass that would permit us to safely reenter the bay immediately outside those protective offshore islands. Working our way south from there, we would eventually be able to rejoin the north-south waterway between the offshore islands and the main coastal mountains. Between Kristiansund and this breakwater, the area immediately offshore as well as the North Sea outside was an impassable confusion of rocks and obstructions. The breakwater at the end of the passage was marked, according to the chart, with two buoys. One, a black buoy with a yellow stripe, defined an impassable end to the breakwater. The other, a yellow buoy with a black stripe, marked the pass.

The wind was on our nose from the south and was rising. We motored into it, making about two or three knots against a thirty-knot blow. The sun was still out, but the seas were now eight to ten feet high and a line of dark clouds hovered on the horizon. If only we could make the buoys, we could slip inside the offshore islets out of danger and work our way down to the entrance to the inner waterway.

As we approached the line of rocks that marked the end of our outer passage, I searched the distance in vain for the two buoys. Finally I spotted a rusted buoy with no markings on it. Which one was it? The seas were striking the rocks in front of us with huge force, driving spray perhaps a hundred feet in the air. Spray and foam hid most of the rocks, and I struggled to find a safe passage. *Free Spirit*'s bow rose and fell with a crash as each of the rolling seas came barreling in, threatening to crush our hull on some unseen ledge beneath. Cindy started to scream out at me to go back, but return was not possible with the storm descending on us, and there was no possibility of finding sea room among all those islets and ledges. I gritted my teeth and concentrated on the task at hand. This was no time to allow fear to control me. At last I discerned a line of quiet water no more than thirty feet wide between the rocks. With my heart in my mouth I drove *Free Spirit* toward the gap with spray flying in our faces from the surrounding turmoil. The wind was now blowing a full gale and the clouds were a solid black wall no more than two miles from us. Shoreward was a solid mass of mountains, and the cut into the fjord was still ten miles farther south. No protected harbor could be seen on the chart.

Suddenly, I saw a sail against the cliffs almost five miles away. As I watched, this sail, one of only five sailboats we were to see on the entire western Norwegian coast, disappeared into the mountains. "Well," I said to Cindy, "If he can go there, so can we." I kept my eye on the spot where he had vanished as if this were a man-overboard drill. As we neared the area, we found poles in the water with arrows on top indicating a local channel. Following the poles, we located a tiny cleft in the rock no more than twenty feet wide. *Free Spirit* has a beam of nearly fourteen feet; this was going to be close. With ten-foot seas behind us, and winds now gusting up to fifty knots, we surfed through the narrow channel and rounded up into a diminutive harbor with a few fishing vessels moored and perhaps a half dozen little houses lining the shore. Our unknown rescuer was nowhere to be seen. We dropped our big seventy-five-pound Herreshoff anchor on its ⅜-inch chain in about twenty-five feet of water and snubbed her down. Within minutes the wind was howling at eighty miles an hour and we were driven below into the cabin.

For three days we lay there, thanking fortune and the powers that had guided us out of the teeth of certain destruction. Three days the wind screamed and clawed at us, but our faithful ground tackle held. For three days, we read, played hearts, ate, and poked our noses out into the turmoil to make sure that our anchor was holding. Never once did we see a soul from the village. It might have been a ghost town in the Mojave desert.

Then, as is the weather's wont in this part of the world, it was suddenly sunny and peaceful again. We cautiously crept out into the cockpit. The storm clouds were still visible, but were spreading their poison northward. Blue sky and white cumulus clouds hung overhead. The sun glinted off the village roofs and the greens of grasses and lichens, low trees and mosses gloried in the warmth of its glow. The browns and grays of the rocks in the surrounding hills and mountains were darkened with rainwater. We hauled anchor at 7:00 A.M. and slipped out the narrow inlet with the sun rising behind us.

CHAPTER 10

Ålesund

We left our little hideaway early on August twelfth with sunshine and no wind, but with storm clouds again to be seen farther south on the horizon and a weather forecast of gale-force winds to come. We had thirty miles to go and at least wanted to make Molde, which offered more civilization than the four or five tiny houses of our current anchorage. We powered firmly into the seas left from the previous storm and on into the lowering clouds. Just as we rounded a sea buoy to head toward Molde, we were struck by wind and rain. The visibility dropped to about half a mile or so as we entered a two-mile-long pass between breakers and rocks on either side. Cindy had the grace not to comment on the lack of visibility, and we held our course by compass and found our way. Having made the turn into Molde, we changed our minds and decided to press on to Ålesund. Rivers of water poured off the cliffs on either side as we powered through the rain. The great, jutting crags rose straight from the waterway, with blackened rocks glistening wet. Twisting and turning as it worked its way between the mainland mountains and the cliffs of the offshore islands, the passage was about a mile wide here. Some smaller islands we passed had heavy tree cover, and others were as barren as Telly Savalas's bald pate. On occasion, a little lighthouse could be seen perched precariously on a rocky promontory. Close attention to piloting was mandatory. Carefully following the chart, we noted each outcropping of rock and each craggy island as we worked our way south. Finally we broke out into a large bay surrounded by tree-covered islands. In front of us was an island with a cluster of houses and other buildings working their way up a hillside. As we made our way into Ålesund's little harbor at 7:00 P.M., the sun broke through the clouds, bathing the hundreds of little islands in our vicinity with a golden cheer. The colors of the three- and four-story peaked-roof houses surrounding the waterfront gleamed in the sun with greens and reds and yellows predominating. These and the modern white stone and steel commercial buildings of the community's downtown area, gave the town a peculiarly Norwegian look, an admixture of eighteenth-century dwellings and twentieth-century business.

Immediately after we tied up to the quay, a pleasant, soft-spoken gentleman in a peacoat, with a round, sunburned face and eyes that crinkled with humor, came by and offered to drive us up to the top of the island's mountain for a view of the town. He was still active in the merchant marine. He said that the nicest thing to happen to him in a foreign port was being shown the town by a local. He wanted to do the same for us. We drove up to a circular restaurant overlooking the town, its harbor, and the surrounding islands. As the sun dropped below the horizon, it framed the scene so that the islands began to appear darkened against a blood red sky. Small toy-size freighters and fishing boats could be seen dawdling up and down the interisland routes, each tracing a wake like contrails across the sky. Food was served cafeteria-style and I had roasted mutton ribs and roasted potatoes, with Drammen cream cakes for dessert. Peter tried some extremely thin, light *pannekake* (pancakes) with a berry sauce. They were delicious and he sold them to the rest of the family, who indulged themselves as well. After dinner, we walked down the steep hill to the streets of Ålesund and worked our way down to the harbor in the gathering dusk.

The next day dawned cold and rainy with gale-force winds. The western coast of Norway is noted for its rainy summers, and their summer season really is the month of July up until the second week of August. We were already pushing it. As we wandered through the streets of downtown Ålesund the night before, Cindy had noticed the sales office of Rank Xerox, the European subsidiary of her company. The next day she went over and spoke with the manager. They had a cup of coffee together and he showed her his machines, the same machines Cindy sold in the States, but with altered paper trays to fit European paper. On her way back to the boat, she encountered a distinguished-looking gentleman named Anton. He, like so many others we met in Norway, was extremely gracious, and volunteered to help us. He drove me to get some engine oil at a filling station and offered us a mooring at a safe harbor in front of his house at the other end of the island. He felt that we should move there for safety's sake as well as conviviality, for the commercial quay in the harbor offered little in the way of protection if a bad storm came through.

Anton was the local real estate court judge and, being a good judge of real estate, he had his own private harbor with just three homes on it, all belonging to members of his family. We did some shopping during the day and late in the afternoon motored to his end of the island. Anton gave us his mooring and tied his boat up to his dock. The harbor was a little bight perhaps a quarter of a mile wide, with a tiny entrance of thirty or forty feet. Numerous private markers led us from an offshore buoy into the haven, for shallow ledges predominated on this end of the island. The land rose quickly from the edge of the harbor past three broad, grassy knolls overlooking the scene. A single mooring sat in the middle of the little bay, and Anton and a woman stood and waved to us from his small wooden dock tucked in on our left. Long, broad, wooden steps climbed a winding path through brush and bushes toward a low-roofed house barely visible on a hill. We rowed over to the dock in our dinghy and shook hands enthusiastically all around. Anton showed us his pride and joy, a thirty-six-foot motorsailer made in Finland. She was handsomely outfitted and he and his wife Anna Lise, a round-faced, substantial woman with a sunny smile and graying hair, thrived on vacation trips to their beloved fjords.

Anna Lise invited us to dinner that night and Anton regaled us with stories of the Norwegian coast. His beautiful twenty-one-year-old daughter, Marie Louise, tall, full-figured, and slim, with very light blond hair, startling blue eyes, and a broad, infectious smile was a law student who had been graciously treated when she was a transfer student in the States. Their son, Jan Erich, was fourteen, with the same blond hair and blue eyes. Like his dad, he was about six feet four. Five-foot Cindy had difficulty standing near them without developing a crick in her neck.

The following day, August fifteenth, was Peter's eighteenth birthday. Anton drove us to a museum where we could see old Norwegian fishing dories and the sod-roofed log cabin houses that used to dominate this coast. The logic of their construction was clear. They were long, low affairs, with the sod providing insulation from the cold winters and the pitch of their roofs designed to shed heavy snow. Ålesund, like Kristiansund, was badly damaged during World War II. The new center of town is a monument to Norwegian resilience. Anton pointed out places where members of the resistance hid out in underground bunkers, broadcasting information about German ship movements with hidden radios. Many local lads had been killed in the war and several had been executed for participating in the resistance.

Anna Lise's dinner that evening was delicious fresh cod. I shared the log of our Atlantic crossing, which appealed to this sea-oriented family. After dinner, we invited everyone down to the boat, where we had a birthday celebration for Peter. Anna Lise brought a beautiful, traditional multilayered Norwegian cake called a *Kransekake* with eighteen candles for the occasion. We all sang "Happy Birthday," apparently an international hit since everyone pitched in with the words and the tune.

We sailed the next day with Anton, Anna Lise, and Jan Erich to the entrance to the Hjørundfjorden (the wild fjord). Anton, tall and slim in his khaki pants and jacket, jaunty with his maritime cap perched over his weather-lined regular features, thoroughly enjoyed handling *Free Spirit*'s wheel as we leaned to the weight of an eighteen-knot breeze. Sunshine and laughter abounded as Jan Erich tried to tell what it was like to be a teenager in Norway, his English not quite as smooth as his father's. Anna Lise, with a lilt and a distinctively Germanic lisp to her consonants, spoke softly of family unity and closeness in their compound by the sea, and described family gatherings in the darkness of winter that managed to dispel the gloom. Anton told us proudly about his daughter's recent entrance to law school at the University of Oslo.

Marie Louisa met us at the ferry landing and took her family back home, leaving us to explore the primordial scenery of the wild fjord. That evening we tied up at a stone quay at the end of a tiny village. Elizabeth and John took off in the dinghy to do some fishing. We had roast pork from our freezer for dinner and we spent a lovely, peaceful night in the fjord.

The next day we motored down the fjord. It was about a mile wide and thirty miles long, plunging into the heart of the mountains. High peaks ahead of us were capped with snow; on either side rose steep cliffs and crags. Little inlets snuck off here and there leading to nowhere. There were no farms, no houses, no sign of human habitation. Whereas elsewhere in fjord country we often saw homes or cottages perched where none seemed possible, here there were none. Within the fjords few if any birds could be seen. No flocks of gulls or terns flew screaming after local fishing boats. Perhaps this is because the local herring fishery had disappeared. Perhaps we simply didn't notice, but I have wracked my mind and questioned my family and no one can remember any birds. (On the open sea, it was much different. Sea birds were present all the way across from Nantucket to Ireland. One had even alighted on our rigging after spending a half hour or so trying to catch the moving spreader. He stayed there all day and was gone the next. We never discovered his fate.) Nor do we remember insects. No flying creatures of any kind decorated or disturbed the scene. Even in the open fish market of Bergen, there were no flies.

The next day we motorsailed to the neighboring Geir-angerfjord. A magnificent, tortuous passage carried us between towering cliffs of rock with green mosses and lichens spreading along the clefts between, and scrub brush and trees making way for the rushing torrents of waterfalls. The water reflected the cliffs in a fabulous collage of browns, grays, and greens. At one point the walls were so close that we could yell and whistle and hear our echoes bouncing off cliffs three and four times. "Hello-ello-ello-lo-o." The inner end of the fjord opened up into a beautiful little bay and a pretty little village surrounded by cliffs. We tied up to the quay and climbed high up on a perch overlooking the fjord. The kids ran themselves ragged, with Peter clowning around pretending to slip over the steep cliff. This harbor was more commercialized, with a couple of large cruise ships anchored in the fjord. The store above the quay offered racks and shelves of beautiful items so we each bought a lovely, handmade Norwegian sweater and had them shipped home.

The following day outdid all the others. We motored to Valldal for our planned rendezvous with Anton and Jan Erich. Anton drove us on a fairyland journey. Long tunnels cut through the mountains were a miracle of engineering. Roughly cut and unfinished, many were so long that they were entirely black within and had to be lit up with our headlights. Most were two lanes, but one was only one lane and an operator at either end with a two-way radio signaled the flow of the light traffic. Eventually, the twisting roads led up to the dam at Tafjord. We got out of the car to look at the enormous architectural marvel. Goats grazed everywhere and Elizabeth, ever the animal lover, soon had a kid cradled in her arms. Near the top of the dam, Anton arranged for us to have a marvelous private trip to the top of the mountain on a cable car used to service the hydroelectric project. From the swaying car, we could see the fjords winding out to the ocean far, far away. The mountain dropped away from our rising car and Cindy gripped my hand. Anton grinned. The kids babbled and leaned over to see how high we were going. Snow and ice graced the mountain's top. Anton picked up some plastic sheets from the sheds and sent the kids sliding on the snow. Elizabeth, always the daredevil, slid away below us, out of control, and barely stopped on the brim of a huge rock. My heart was in my mouth as I screamed for her to be careful. She looked at me as if to say, "Oh, dad!" and I fell silent. The crispness of the air, the bite of the gentle breeze, the brightness of the sun, all etched the scene permanently in my memory.

Anton then took us to a small hotel at Tafjord. The tiny inn, nestled in a little valley in the foothills of the mountains was built partly of logs and partly of wood-frame construction. With a low, pitched roof and broad bay windows, it had a dining room capable of seating perhaps thirty people. Bright sunshine streamed in through dormers overhead. A friendly proprietress in her early thirties greeted us as we filed in. Several tables were filled with local diners, but Anton spoke quietly to her and she shortly found us a table for seven. A waitress in a long traditional festive dress waited on us and served us with a shy smile. We had an absolutely smashing lunch of smoked salmon, homemade bread, fresh salad greens from their own garden, sour cream, hot roast beef, potatoes, vegetables, and a delicious sweet and sour dessert of fresh, local mountain berries called *tyttebaer*. This was followed by *rondecrem*, a gelatin dish with sugar, cream, and peaches. Delicious!

After dinner, no check came to the table; Anton indicated that it was all taken care of. We sat around with our coffee and lounged back against the comfortable, rounded wooden chairs, unwilling to disturb our overfilled bellies. Eventually, Anton indicated that he had more to show us, so we trekked outside into the bright sun. It took more than a few moments for our eyes to become accustomed to the glare. I looked around and took in the rich, verdant setting of fields and forests with a grassy track for a road wending its way through the nearby hills. The mountains in the distance seemed painted on the sky like the backdrop scenery for a theatrical performance. Here and there, small birds could be seen pecking around cow dung and a fallen-down fence in the distance marked the limits of an over-grown field of hay.

During dinner, Elizabeth had expressed amazement that we could see farmhouses near the entrance to Geiranger-fjord. These clung to the side of the mountains and seemed totally isolated from any form of civilization. No road could be seen leading to them and no other houses or villages were present for miles. Situated 2,500 feet or so up the mountain, their only connection with the outside appeared to be a rope pulley connected to an ancient piling near the edge of the fjord. Often a small rowing skiff or a little powerboat would lie just offshore on the end of a short line, bobbing in the breeze. "How do those people live?" the kids wanted to know.

Anton took us to see a 600-year-old farm overlooking one of the fjords. A dirt road that had been cut into the side of the mountain led us there. The owner, an 84-year-old farmer, and his equally aging wife had been a clients of Anton's prior to his sitting on the court. They still took care of goats and other farm animals, but invited young people from elsewhere in Europe to spend time on their farm and work the gardens. Some young German girls were staying with them when we visited, and they showed us the barn, the hay fields, and the cattle and goats that contributed to their subsistence. Many of the farms we saw were apparently empty. It was no longer economically feasible for them to operate.

As the day started to wane, Anton took us to his cabin in the mountains. A well-built, handsome, rustic-looking log cabin with a sod roof like those built in the old style, it was charming and comfortable inside; with large over-stuffed chairs and sofa, a fine little kitchen, and two bedrooms off the living room. It had no electricity or running water. We joined Anton in a short walk to a mountain spring nearby where we drew fresh, clear, delicious water by the bucket. Kerosene lamps and candles cast a soft glow as evening descended and a fire in the huge fireplace in the sitting room roared and crackled.

A venison dinner was prepared over a wood-burning stove to complete our day's delight. When Anton finally took us back to *Free Spirit*, the kids bubbled over in their excitement and wonder about the day. Cindy and I whispered together, "How can we repay his wonderful hospitality?" We had not carried presents with us in the limited lockers of the boat and I was able to give Anton but a small token from our cruising library, Don Street's classic, *The Ocean-sailing Yacht*, as a thank-you and remembrance from the crew of *Free Spirit*. This generous and gracious man still corresponds with us at Christmastime, and we hope to see him and his beautiful country again some day.

The following day, August twentieth, we heard that our request for an extension to our customs permit to allow *Free Spirit* to remain in Norway over the winter for repairs had been approved. Heading back toward Ålesund, we motored and sailed from Valldal past the farmhouse where we had spent part of the previous day. On the dock as we passed by, the German girls and a neighbor waved enthusiastically. We waved in return.

A security call over the VHF indicated that a force eight to nine gale was due that afternoon. We barely had time to put on our foul-weather gear before it hit. The blast struck us like a huge fist and we powered into it to find a protected harbor at Hareid. Coming into a commercial dock, I almost lost Cindy against the concrete pier. We had to motor with more speed than we preferred to overcome the force of the gale. As we approached the high side of the quay, fully eight feet above our decks, Cindy hung out to grab a ladder and climb it with a docking line. The rain blew in at an angle as the wind gusted again. I threw the engine into reverse without totally throttling back in order to back in to the pier. The feathering prop did not engage and we did not go into reverse. I swung the wheel hard over to port, missing the dock by inches, and Peter threw his shoulder into the cement quay to help us off. Elizabeth leaped from the bow to grab her mother's arm and pull her back. Cindy wiggled out from her position between the shrouds and the concrete jetty just in time to avoid being knocked off into the water, and we blew off the dock to try for a safer landing. We finally rafted to an old, uninhabited wreck of a commercial sailing coaster, and spent the day fixing bilge and water pumps. That evening we ate half the salmon that Anton had given us for our freezer. The next day we would start the long trek south for Bergen.

Family and friends gather to wish us bon voyage.

Dolphins accompany our second attempt.

My first effort at homemade bread.

Only John can fit in the anchor
locker to seal the leak.

Peter learning celestial navigation.

Our crew acts up during a gale at sea.

Sunsets at sea can be
magnificent.

The skipper and his mate behind the twins.

Landfall at Fastnet Rock.

Ireland, a land of misty beauty.

The kids and their friends in Baltimore Harbor.

Private garden in Glengariff.

John's eleventh birthday
en route to Norway.

Elizabeth is her usual irrepressible self.

Med delfiner og blåhai over Atlanteren:

Seiler-drømmen virkelig

Our arrival in Norway is heralded in the local press.

Mountainous terrain of the Norwegian fjords.

The haunting beauty of a wild fjord.

Free Spirit peacefully allows us to fish in the fjords.

View of Ålesund harbor from a restaurant overlooking the town.

Norwegian farm at the edge of the fjord.

Anton explains ancient Norwegian home construction to us.

Peter's birthday in Ålesund. Cindy, Marie Louise, Peter, John, Anton, Anna Lise, Elizabeth, and Jan Erich.

The farm in the mountains far above the fjord.

Kids sledding on the mountains high above the fjord.

The author relaxing after a climb to the heights above Geirangerfjord.

Peter, Bob, John, and Cindy overlooking Geirangerfjord.

The entry to Geirangerfjord narrows considerably.

Dinner for twelve aboard *Free Spirit* in Målöy.

Bergen, its Hanseatic heritage showing in its architecture.

Refuge for the Norwegian navy.

Fog rolls in and envelops us in the soup.

Fall cruising in Norway.

Prehistoric monster? No. An oil rig on the North
Sea seen at night.

Danish sail-training vessel en route to Scotland.

Balmoral Castle, summer palace of the queen.

Harbor crow at Cowes, Admiral Cup week.

Philippe and Joel flank Cindy.

Port Manech—Philippe's magnificent riverside summer home.

Breton town (Port Aven) on holiday.

CHAPTER 11

Målöy

Our voyage now was to take us down long stretches of lightly inhabited waterways, past small villages, and eventually out again into the open North Sea. Farther south the mountains of the coast are somewhat lower than they are near Ålesund, their surfaces bare except for greenish scrub brush. At unexpected intervals, enterprising farmers have planted trees to forest large tracts of otherwise barren islands. The real surprise for me was the degree of habitation. Norway is a long country with only four million inhabitants, yet every reasonable and many a totally unreasonable spot is inhabited or at least has a structure of some sort on it. Every valley between the mountains has its cluster of houses, a village, or a township. In between, variously placed on level areas near the shore or precariously balanced on mountain ledges are small farms with surrounding green patches of cultivation such as the one we visited near Ålesund.

Every island large enough to hold a house or farm does so. Little white lighthouses with orange pointed roofs dot the prominent land edges. Mountains rise on either side in the fjords, more steeply and awesomely in the interior fjords, more gently along the outer coast.

The weather is cool. Sun, not the rarity the natives claim in the summer of 1982, shows bright and clear but low in the sky. The rains when they come, with their accompanying southwest winds, can be associated with fierce and sudden gales of surprising force. Force seven, eight, and nine storms are relatively common. This can make travel for the small boat somewhat risky. With the long stretches between protected harbors on certain parts of the coast, the innumerable rocks and islets, and the absence of a numbering system or a sufficient quantity of buoys, long voyages in this area are not for the neophyte sailor.

Dependence on sophisticated radio-navigational devices is chancy. We found our usually reliable Loran C off by as much as thirty miles on the coast north of Bergen. The mountains that dominate the region bend and deflect the radio waves, resulting in distortions. Satellite fixes retained their usual accuracy, but with updated positions given only every six to eight hours, seldom gave the pinpoint positioning needed to work one's way between two rows of underwater rocks with no adjacent buoys. The frequently overcast skies rule out reliance on sunsights and only very careful pilotage, with close attention paid to each offshore island or promontory, can bring one safely to port. We found that fog was seldom of a magnitude to startle a New Englander during the summer, but became quite dense on occasion during September. Mostly, it was a heavy mist that reduced visibility to a half mile or so.

The charts seem quite accurate, but a magnifying lens is essential, since many of the details are only visible with magnification. The native Norwegian charts are better than the ones produced by the U.S. Hydrographic Office, but are more difficult to come by in the States. Chart names are confusing too, since Norway is blessed with three different languages, all of which are taught in school. Ancient Norwegian, no longer spoken, is preserved for the sake of tradition. Regional Norwegian is spoken in many different small towns and has an infinite variety of nuances and lilts, each peculiar to its own valley. Official Norwegian is spoken in Oslo and the larger cities and is largely the result of many centuries of Danish rule. The charts, as a result, may have different names given to the same island, town or city, fjord, or promontory depending on who drew up the chart. This can make going from one chart to the next confusing, since one has to concentrate on the shapes of various land masses rather than the names for quick identification.

Weather in the fjords is quite changeable. Many fjords are fairly large bodies of water and the wind sometimes swept down suddenly off a mountainside, even on a nice day, and sent us charging along with our rail under. This, on a sixteen-ton sloop that is quite stiff and stable, was exhilarating. On a smaller boat, a dangerous broach or capsize could occur.

Windshifts are also frequent, and can be frustrating. We had to be alert so that dangerous and unintentional jibes did not occur. Despite the twists and turns in the fjords, the tendency of the wind to follow the course of a fjord as it is funneled down meant that we frequently found it on our nose no matter which direction we seemed to be heading. This forced us to proceed under power a great deal of the time. Distances, for a New Englander, seem surprisingly long, and the steady, reliable six knots produced by the engine made pilotage and arrival in safe harbor more of a certainty.

Numerous ferries connecting nowhere with everywhere constantly ply the waters and, at times appear almost as if by magic. Many freighters and fishing boats go up and down the waterways, but despite this the overwhelming feeling one gets is a civilized solitude with long miles between occasional watercraft.

The second day out of Hareid, the sky was an incredible blue with occasional white, fleecy fair-weather clouds that looked to be lying peacefully at anchor. The water in the fjord showed only a slight ripple with a gentle breeze off our port bow. We were powering toward Stadlandet, enjoying complete peace and relaxation. The ever-changing shapes of the land around us, and the need to change course around some islet occasionally, added interest. (Our autopilot was certainly of much greater value in Norway than a wind vane would have been.) Music filled the cockpit. The seductive melodies of Grieg's *Peer Gynt Suite* seemed perfect for this lovely day. Cindy read Leo Buscaglia's *Love* to a sunbathing Peter. The grace and loveliness of the words washed over us in rhythm with the music. *Free Spirit* floated in a sea of feathery foam as she glided like a ballerina across the mirrorlike fjord.

After a brief overnight stay tied to a decaying, unoccupied pier, we set off south again. The sun had decided to take another holiday. Stadlandet, thrusting out twelve miles to the northwest like a dragon's head, blocks the passage down the interisland waterway. The long slog around it involved an outside route in one of those areas of the coast not protected by a row of offshore islands. Because it is so exposed to the violence of the North Sea, and because it is a lee shore in southerly gales, Stadlandet has a fearsome reputation in the area, but relatively calm conditions blessed us. We tucked into the inner waterway again and scooted down to a small fishing town called Må-löy I had thought of it as an interim anchorage on the way to Bergen. We planned one night. We stayed a week.

Målöy is a town of about two thousand inhabitants on an island with a total of perhaps five thousand people. We pulled in around eight in the evening. (I would ordinarily say "at night," but night didn't start to fall in late August until well after midnight this far north.) We found a berth in a vacant slip along the quay and settled down to plan some supper.

Shortly after we had secured our lines, we noticed a man in a dark sweater and fisherman's hat walking slowly along the edge of the quay staring at our boat. I poked my head out of the companionway and called, "Hello." He nodded in response and I followed up with, "Would you like to come below and have a glass of wine?" He seemed to straighten and open up at this, but hesitated, unsure of my sincerity. "Come on aboard," I volunteered. "We are just opening a bottle of wine and some cheese—and I'm sure you'd like to see our boat." Well, that did it. He smiled, introduced himself, and stepped aboard. Of medium build and with a dark, heavy, close-shaven beard, Gunnar quickly became quite talkative. Like so many others, he was intrigued by our adventure. He owned a shipyard about five miles up the coast, and although he dealt largely with commercial vessels, he was in the process of building himself a sailboat. He asked if he could bring his wife aboard and disappeared, soon to return with an attractive, tall, dark-haired woman. Evelyn was as interesting as her husband. They begged us to delay our dinner hour and asked us to excuse them for an hour or so. When they returned, they came with an invitation for us to join them at a friend's house.

All seven of us piled into Gunnar's four-seater sedan. We drove down the main road parallel to the water, then turned left to head up a steep hill. Houses, mostly of frame construction, clustered together as if for warmth. The narrow streets and alleys could barely accommodate the little car. A series of lefts and rights and we were at our destination. A newly remodeled home set on a modest quarter-acre of land greeted us. Formal columns decorated the entrance and a patch of lawn gave color to the front yard.

Jon and his wife, Grethe, owners of a local store were our hosts. Their home built a century earlier, had been periodically enlarged in later years and had recently acquired a massive new addition, culminating in its current grace and style. As we entered the house, which had belonged to Jon's grandfather, we stepped into a spacious white marble foyer leading into a large entry hall. A spiral staircase led upstairs. We ate in an enormous dining room, some thirty-five feet long, with a grand oak table and a suit of armor guarding the doorway. Jon and Grethe's friends Jan and Solfrid, Svein and Karin, and Gunnar and Evelyn shared our table. We dined royally, entertained with local tales, and in turn we spun many a yarn of our adventures at sea.

The following day Gunnar took us on a tour of the island and of his shipyard. He offered to help us find someone to repair our bowsprit and the foredeck, a major concern for us. His own yard dealt mostly with commercial vessels and in steel, but he felt that we could find local storage for the boat for the winter, which would be reliable and inexpensive, and that repairs could be arranged.

The next day, a Sunday, Evelyn and Gunnar invited us to their house for dinner. They had a young son John's age. He spoke little English, but enjoyed playing games with John.

Gunnar had made some contacts in a town about fifteen miles north, where he'd found someone who was willing and able to store and repair our boat. So we sailed to the town to meet the man—I'll call him Edvard—who was to assist us over the next ten months. There we found a beautiful, protected little bay with a quiet nook, surrounded by trees, in which Edvard felt *Free Spirit* could lie safely for the winter. He would drop a mooring for us and work on the fiberglass in the spring.

Without any definite commitments made, we left and soon saw another yacht hull down on the horizon. This was very unusual; yachting and sailing are relatively unknown in these waters. It was a thirty-four-foot sloop owned by a friend of Gunnar's named Arve. At the time, I had just put a steak on our charcoal grill on the rail and was about to start preparing dinner. Arve invited us to his little harbor and soon the whole crowd was there. Grethe and Jon and their kids, Svein, Gunnar, a fellow named Ken, and all their wives. Dinner was our steak and several large fish baked in ovens in the ground. We sang songs until one in the morning, when most of the guests left. Arve was irrepressible, however, and Cindy and I and our kids were having such a good time that we stayed until 4:00 A.M. Arve was quite a talented musician and played both the trumpet and the piano. I pitched in with piano solos and singing and Cindy, with memories of her days with her college singing group, lent harmony to our blends. In the wee hours, we stumbled back to *Free Spirit* in the pitch dark with the assistance of a borrowed flashlight.

After sleeping late, we motored the ten or so miles back to Målöy. Again Jon and Grethe had us over for dinner, and again, we were up till late hours singing. The next day, Gunnar sent a diver and an engineer from his yard to check our prop and engine because of a shimmy it had developed at high revolutions. He refused to charge us, even though he was paying the men's salary. Norwegian children begin the school year in August. The children of our new friends called at the boat and asked our kids if they would like to join them. John and Peter jumped at the chance. Elizabeth, of course, would not be left behind, so they all trooped off. They came back aflutter with the experience of being the only foreign children in class. The teachers asked for their participation and they found themselves the center of attention. John was delighted that he could help the teacher with some words in the English class. He found that they were ahead of him in math, however, and he got lost with square roots. Peter and Elizabeth, of course, were taken to the high school. All the students sat in one class and the teachers came in to them. They talked about politics and the differences between socialism and capitalism. "Only one of the students smoked," Elizabeth reported, "and everyone was in great shape. They all went to the track together and ran for exercise and fun. One of the things that struck me about the Norwegian teens, both in Kristiansund and Målöy, was how serious and grown up they seemed. They appeared to have serious purposes and goals in their lives, and to know where they were headed."

That night, we invited everyone to *Free Spirit* for a dinner prepared by our own chef. I cooked two pork roasts in our little oven to serve as the entrée in a multicourse meal complete with champagne and wine. For the first time we had dinner for twelve aboard. At the end of the dinner Jan rose and toasted us with appreciation for our visit and hospitality. They had all chipped in to give us presents, a Helly Hansen wool knit jacket for Cindy, a captain's badge and a real and rare Norwegian sea captain's hat for the skipper. All our guests signed the brim to engrave the moment in our memories.

One of the very nicest things about living in Norway is the closeness of community life. Everyone sees his neighbors frequently at work, in daily activities, at play, and through the children, so it is not surprising to see them develop close friendships. Each person is dependent upon his neighbor. The whole community tries to protect each and everyone's job. Gunnar told us that it is impossible to fire someone once he has been hired. You must try to help him get on in his position or else give him a job he is capable of doing. The community is also concerned with larger issues. If the fishing industry is hurt, the whole community is deeply affected. When the herring disappeared a few years ago, and the cod and salmon were gone, the town council met and decided on a new course of action: They would catch dogfish, which were plentiful, and sell them abroad as "rock salmon," a delicacy.

There are only four million Norwegians and they have a strong sense of national identity. Although everyone complains about taxes, which are high, the standard of living is also high. Expensive European and Japanese cars were commonplace and housing appeared in generally good condition. Oil revenues from the North Sea fields, of course, have contributed to their prosperity.

The next day we tore ourselves away to head to Florø. Everywhere we went in Norway, Norwegians warned us to be careful of other Norwegians. They were "cold and distant," "unfriendly," "did not like strangers." From our reception in Kristiansund and Ålesund, and now in Målöy, and from our later experiences all the way from Bergen to the little island of Espevaer, we found only warm, kind, friendly folk. Even the skippers of commercial vessels often waved, and one blue 100-foot freighter, the *Solfjord*, slowed down as she passed us so her skipper could come out of the wheelhouse to wave hello. We owe a debt of gratitude to these people. They made us feel that western Norway was our home.

CHAPTER 12

Rain

The wind blows harsh across the hills
And down the mountainsides.
It funnels up the fjords and blows
Spray thrown into our eyes.

*W*estern Norway is known for its astounding annual rainfall. Bergen must be the rain capitol of the north. We had some beautiful, sunny days while in Norway; the summer of 1982 was one of the better summers on that coast. The summer, however, is brief, lasting until the second week of August. Then come the rains. We had already experienced several days of showers and downpours, including two while in Målöy. On August twenty-sixth we left for Florø. It rained off and on for much of the day. Squalls buffeted us, followed by relatively peaceful periods with beautiful rainbows appearing, sometimes one on top of another. On a few occasions, we even saw three rainbows at a time. Profuse and exuberant waterfalls limned mountainous terrain.

As we approached the narrows leading to Florø, we were suddenly struck by a force nine gale with rain so heavy that it totally obliterated all vision even of the bow of our boat. We were, at that point, in a narrow cut with rocks on either side. One minute I had vision and the next we were completely blinded. I rushed to the radar, which had been on standby, and flipped the switch. The radar was totally blinded by the rain too. Back at the wheel, I tried to guide the boat by the compass and the memory I retained as to what the channel had looked like prior to the storm. Meanwhile, the heavy gale-force winds were trying to drive us backward, and seas were beginning to form. It was too deep to anchor and we couldn't see the rocks. I kept the throttle at 1500 RPMs to barely hold steerage way against the storm and somehow, with luck, managed to clear the rocks. We opened out into a large bay near the island of Florø as the heavens drew their breath, and managed to con our way into the harbor before the storm struck with renewed rage. We lay at a commercial quay for the next twenty-four hours while the storm's fury beat at us. The rains were so heavy that we chose not to leave the cabin and never saw much of Florø.

The following morning, the rain had eased and the skies had lightened. By eight o'clock the sun was occasionally breaking out of the clouds and Peter and I cast off our lines. We were anxious to get down to Bergen, which would be likely to have larger boatyards to do our repairs. We were somewhat unsure of the situation near Målöy. As we motored out of the harbor, we could see fishing and commercial craft heading in from all directions. A leaden sky faced off against us. We, of course, kept going—and ran right into the vicious blast of a cold front.

The darkened skies dealt us icy force eight to nine winds and stinging rain. Visibility was again totally blotted out, so we turned tail and scooted back into the harbor. We tied up for two hours until the worst had passed, and then headed out again. We motored twenty miles in intermittent squalls and persistent rain. The wind blew constantly at thirty-five to forty knots with higher gusts on our nose all the way. We finally pulled into a little harbor about four in the afternoon. We anchored, and I fell asleep from exhaustion.

The following day dawned as bad as the previous two. To me this was unbelievable. Storms in New England are generally of short duration. We may have rainy weather for three or four days, but the periods of heavy winds and storm conditions usually last no more than a few hours. This was now our third day of gale-force winds blowing at forty knots or higher. We had anchored close to shore in a little bight of a large harbor under the lee of the land. The wind had shifted from the southeast to the southwest during the night and it became apparent that if it shifted any more, we could be blown on shore. At 1:30 A.M. I got up, dressed warmly, put on boots and foul-weather gear, and rowed out a second anchor to the northwest. I used the little twenty-two-pound high-tensile Danforth that I had bought ten years earlier as the storm anchor for my first cruising boat, *Little Dove*. We rode well between the two anchors as the wind shifted around to the west. At ten the next morning, it was still blowing like hell. Even as well protected as we were, a slight swell and some wave action developed.

We decided to weigh anchor. I stepped on the control button. Cindy waited on the helm, our big diesel purring reassuringly. The winch lay silent. I hit the button again. No comforting whirr. The moan of the wind in the rigging kept up its incessant roar and now seemed to mock my feeble efforts. Again and again I hit the switch. Damn thing, it must be broken. I looked around at the isolated little pond where we sat; at the surrounding mountains, which appeared unassailable; at the darkened sky, which seemed to deny us access to God; and I sat down in complete capitulation to the fates. This was it. There was no way that we could raise 900 pounds of anchor and chain sixty feet to the surface of the fjord. We were stuck. Either I would have to jettison chain and anchor worth $1,500 or we would be pinned there forever.

I called the family below for a conference. Cindy pointed out that if we dropped the big anchor where we lay, we had no reliable backup for the rocky bottoms we now seemed to find every night. There was no way that our forty-five-pound CQR on its line and chain would hold reliably under the conditions we now faced. The big Herreshoff and its 200 feet of chain were vital. Peter went on deck to try the switch. Perhaps it would suddenly work now. It didn't. Well, now it was time to become an electrician.

I've feared electricity since I was sixteen years old and tried to repair a switch for my father in his office. Dad was a physician too, a general practitioner with his own office in Boston. The switch operated a high current-drawing sterilizer. After the repair, I flipped the switch on and stood riveted to the floor of his office, gaping with amazement as flames flashed around my hand. My father took one look and leaped across the office, striking me at the waist with a football tackle to knock me away from the device. My hand was blackened, the skin charred, and it stayed that way for weeks. Ever since then, I have maintained a shocked respect for electrical repairs. Now, however, was not the time to be paralyzed by the past.

I had Peter, my on-deck assistant, activate the foot switch over and over. Using a screwdriver to create a brief short, I found that we had power up to a relay under the deck, but no power beyond that relay. I took the relay out of the system. Examining it on the cabin table, I observed that it had been welded together at the factory and was obviously not meant to be taken apart for repairs. Unfortunately, we had no spare. I took a hacksaw and cut it in half. Examining the interior, I discovered that it was a spring-loaded device that closed when a current was applied to one of its contacts. Unfortunately, a plastic insulator appeared to have melted from overheating and the relay had shorted out. I took a thick piece of plastic from the tool drawer and cut out a new insulator to fit. I then reconstructed the device and taped it together with adhesive tape. It looked like an injured war victim returning to duty from a M.A.S.H. facility when I reinstalled it into the system. With my heart in my mouth, I called to Peter to hit the switch again. Eureka, it worked!

On the afternoon of August twenty-eighth, we fought the two anchors aboard at 1:00 P.M. and motored with the wind on our nose at twenty-five to thirty knots. Intermittent rain and cold air faced us. We could see our breath on the air. We were in wild and empty country now. The mountains rose up steeply on either side of the two-mile-wide fjord. No anchorages were to be found on the chart, so I finally turned into a little cut in the rock that led through a narrow, winding passage into a completely isolated pond about a half mile in diameter, encircled by high mountains. The chart gave no depths and we motored around the entire little bay with no bottom showing on our deep-sea sounder. Finally, only 250 feet from shore, we spotted an area of bottom at a depth of 90 feet. As we traced it toward shore, it shallowed to about 30 feet about 20 feet off the rocky beach. The wind had finally died and the skies had cleared after one last soaking rain. We dropped the bow anchor in 40 feet of water about 75 feet from shore and let out our entire 250 feet of anchor rode plus 15 feet of chain on the forty-five-pound CQR. We backed down toward deep water and dropped the seventy-five-pound Herreshoff in 90 feet of water with its 200 feet of chain out. We could hear the anchor scraping on the solid rock below us, but the trusty Herreshoff grabbed onto a rocky outcropping and held firm.

This little harbor was the most isolated we had been to yet, a little bay off the small throughway fjord along which we had been traveling. There was no habitation anywhere near, and surrounded as it was by snow-capped peaks, we could not get, nor presumably transmit, any radio signals. Isolated outcroppings of rocks and small islets dotted the far end of the bay, and it was nearly a mile in from the main fjord. If we had problems here, we would probably not be found for months. The situation reminded me of the one described by Myles and Beryl Smeeton on the Patagonian coast of South America. As they make plain in *Because the Horn Is There*, shipwreck on an isolated coast is unlikely to allow rescue. The rains had resumed, but we felt fortunate that at least for now the wind had died.

I went to bed that night with a granddaddy of a cold. We slept fitfully until 3:00 A.M., when I got up to check our anchors. I had dropped the big Herreshoff with a float attached to act as a trip line. Unfortunately, the trip line was only about sixty feet long and the anchor dropped into ninety feet of water. I had visions of fouling the big anchor and being unable to raise it with my damaged bowsprit, which could only take a reasonable amount of strain despite my previous repairs. That night I had nightmares of getting lost below the surface in the darkness of the fjord as I tried, in scuba gear, to locate the trip line.

At 6:45 A.M. I awoke to the moaning of the wind. As I pulled on my long underwear and foul-weather gear, I glanced at the sky. Last night's brief fair weather had been but a moment's respite between weather systems, and new storm clouds were racing by. I turned out on deck with a box of Kleenex and a bottle of acetone. The family slept on blissfully, unaware of my concerns. The windlass had been slipping the previous night; I planned to take it apart to clean the brake pads.

I struggled with the big anchor and its chain and had most of the chain into the locker when, with the anchor off the bottom, we started to swing rapidly toward shore. Peter, who had gotten up after hearing all the noise on deck, started the engine, put her in reverse, and kept us off the rocks as I continued to haul up anchor. We could see the stock of the anchor thirty feet below the surface when Murphy's Law intervened. Whoever old man Murphy was, I pray that he fries in everlasting damnation for inventing the curse that has, ever since, tortured us poor sailors. Sixteen feet below our bowsprit and about ten feet above the anchor, the ⅜-inch chain was knotted in a bunch the size of a large grapefruit. There was no way that we could bring that aboard through the bow roller and windlass. We retrieved the floating trip line marker, which had by now surfaced, and hauled the seventy-five pound anchor and equivalent weight of chain aboard by hand. On deck, we were eventually able to untangle the snarl. We put the Herreshoff to bed, hauled in our second anchor, and took off into the gray, blustery southeaster. It was, of course, right on our nose as usual.

That day we had an absolutely brutal drive down the long Fedjefjord into the teeth of a twenty-five-knot wind with three- to four-foot seas. We pounded under power at three to four knots. It was very frustrating to know that had the wind been from astern, we could be making eight knots. With twenty more miles to go as the late afternoon dusk descended, we trudged on our way.

CHAPTER 13

Bergen

*B*ergen, the capital of Norway in the Middle Ages, controlled by Germanic interests, has been a seagoing port from time out of mind. The rain poured straight down heavily, with the intensity that one associates with the tropics, only it was a cold rain, the kind that gets in under your foul-weather gear and penetrates to the marrow. The downpour obliterated the outlines of the harbor as we crept in. At seven in the evening we tied our lines to the harbormaster's dock. The rain continued unabated and I alternated calling out instructions to Peter, Elizabeth, and Cindy with spasms of sneezes as I tried to ignore the cold that was causing me to burn inside almost as much as I was freezing outside. As we attempted to fit fenders between our topsides and the heavy tires lashed to the quay, a Frenchman named Paul suggested that we move our boat to the opposite quay, which would be less exposed to harbor wash and wind action. He offered to move his boat forward to make some room for us.

It was there that we met Philippe, the captain, and his gallant crew: Joel and his sister Chantelle, Pierre, Paul, and Antoine. They invited us to see their boat, a Nicholson 48, and later that night, they invited us for dinner. They had just returned from a voyage to Spitsbergen, the most northerly permanent habitation in the world. (A year later we were to see pictures of their boat amid icebergs, polar bears, and glaciers.) After many a rollicking sea story, I was beginning to collapse from exhaustion and the ravages of my cold. We therefore made our apologies. I loaded up on vitamin C and fluids and went to bed. The next night, we had them all to *Free Spirit*, where we again had dinner for twelve and embellished on our earlier narrations.

Our friend Lolo in Kristiansund had given us the name of a contact, Øystein, who might be able to assist us in finding a place to get repairs and a boatyard where *Free Spirit* could spend the winter.

Reserved by nature, Øystein nevertheless put himself out to take us around to visit some marina facilities around Bergen. Unfortunately, there were no boatyards there where we could get repairs. We invited him and his wife, Byerg over for dinner and spent a pleasant evening.

Meanwhile, our three youngsters, whose sole measure of a successful vacation is how many layers of tan can be accumulated, decided that enough was enough. With school scheduled to start soon, they made the decision to leave Norway eleven days earlier than planned. As marvelous an experience as our summer had been, the past two weeks of rain had rather dampened their enthusiasm for the cruising life. I figured that it must have been pretty bad for them to want to get back to school on time. We had originally planned for them to return to the classroom a week late in order to maximize our experience. It was with some pride that we watched them gather up all their belongings in seabags and confidently take off on an adventure of their own to return to Boston. Two rather long plane rides and two customs declarations later, they arrived as scheduled, and we were relieved to reach them by phone at home. It only remained for us now to find a winter resting place for *Free Spirit* and we could join them.

The fish market in Bergen, right at the foot of our dock, was most remarkable. Every weekday morning at about ten, stalls and tents were set up in a vast, empty, rectangular area bordering the harbor. Arrayed on tables would appear, as if by magic, a wonderfully intriguing and varied smorgasbord of pelagic delights. The fish, shrimp, clams, and other delicacies were unbelievably fresh and delicious. It was hard to get our fill.

Øystein and Bjerg invited us for dinner and introduced us to reindeer as a culinary delight. Børge, a naval architect and a friend of Øystein, recommended a protected harbor on the island of Espevaer and suggested that it had a good yard to do our repairs. We decided to sail south the hundred miles or so to explore the possibilities.

We topped our tanks at a fuel dock, and while there were invited aboard a Norwegian naval frigate. The officer in charge was also the senior officer in charge of training for the Norwegian navy. He offered us coffee and cakes and described his dream of retiring with his wife to a small sailboat just to go cruising. We traded sea stories, and shortly he sent for and gave us a ream of Norwegian charts featuring far greater details of the fjords than did our American charts. With both vessel and crew fueled up, and warmed by the friendship of the Norwegian navy, we cast off and headed south. About two hours later, our navy friends passed by close aboard and gave us a military salute by firing their handguns in the air. They then gave us a hand salute that I returned, very proud to be able to do so in the Norwegian sea captain's hat I had been given in Målöy. Their ship steamed by us and disappeared into a huge cavelike opening in the side of a mountain, marked restricted to military vessels on our chart.

It continued to rain off and on with occasional heavy showers. The wind was on our nose, but gradually freed enough for us to motorsail with our genoa. Thus liberated from the constraints of a dead beat, our speed soon picked up to seven, then eight, and finally eight and a half knots. As we sailed on, I got the bright idea to put up our cockpit awning, which had been designed for the tropics. This allowed us to sail with the genoa and kept much of the rain off us.

We finally made Espevaer at 8:30 P.M. We had a delicious salmon steak dinner that night. Now, of course, it was only Cindy and I. The boat was quiet. We slept in till about ten and awoke to find ourselves in a pretty and well-protected little harbor. Espevaer is a small fishing village on an island in a tiny cluster of islands off the coast of Norway near Haugesund.

We asked about for the man whose name had been given to us in Bergen. We were led to his shed. He spoke no English, but with a young lad acting as translator, he explained that he could shelter the boat for us for the winter, but, after examining the damage, said that he could not repair it. He did not have the expertise, and did not know anyone in the area who did. This meant that we would have to return to Målöy for the repairs, since the man I call Edvard was the only one willing to undertake the job. We did not look forward to the long, 200-mile slog back north. We started to head out to sea to go offshore to Målöy, but the weather gods were perverse. For the past 200 miles, we had been in southerly winds of gale force associated with the storms that had whistled around us. Now, paradoxically, when we had to go north, the weather and the winds shifted. The sun was out and twenty-five-knot winds blew in from the north. We were met by ten-foot seas on our nose and quickly became debilitated by seasickness. After two hours of struggle, we turned back and headed back in to Espevaer to lick our wounds and reconsider our choices. We might have taken medication, but after being on the boat continuously for three months, it never occurred to us that we could still be prone to the affliction. Once the malady hits, of course, it's too late. Medication must be taken early as a preventive.

While we were tied up at the town quay, two teenaged boys came by to talk with us. Shortly, they asked us if we would like to see where a UFO had landed. Since we had no other plans that day, we said "Sure." They took us in a powerboat to an outlying island. The story they told us was that a bright green glow had settled over Espevaer one night five years earlier. It could not be investigated safely in the dark, but the next day the fishermen went out to the area that had been glowing and found, on this islet, a large oval area about the size of a football field where all the grass had been burnt off, leaving bare ground compressed as if something enormously heavy had landed on it. The egg-shaped depression that remained was visible to us from the hilltop we climbed.

It was early to bed that night. The next morning, September fifth, we left early for Målöy and Edvard's nearby harbor. Locals indicated that we could expect the wind to be quiet in the early morning, but that it would pick up by ten and be howling by noon. It was expected to remain in the north. We decided against an offshore beat into the teeth of a howling north wind. September in Norway is really wintery even to my New England blood. We dressed in nearly every thing we owned. I wore two pair of long underwear, two pairs of dungarees, foul-weather pants, T-shirt, long underwear top, long-sleeved jersey, wool shirt, two heavy wool sweaters, a foul-weather jacket, an Orlon neck protector, an Orlon ski hat, a lambswool outer hat, wool mittens, rubber mittens over the wool ones, cotton socks, light wool socks, plastic baggies, heavy wool socks, and foul-weather boots. Despite all that gear, I was still cold.

Even though we were in the "dry" northerly wind, sun showers were still frequent. But instead of the heavy, continuous rain with total overcast, we had a partly cloudy sky with breaks of sunshine and intermittent lighter showers. We kept the awning up and appreciated its added benefit in helping to keep us dry.

I believe that attitude is important to passage-making. I had become seasick the previous day because of rough weather, but also because I was upset that Espevaer could not handle our repairs and we had to make the long return trip. If I had been relaxed, I would probably have been less prone to seasickness.

On September sixth we awoke to a beautiful, clear dawn. The sun rose like a sigh on our peaceful anchorage. The yellows and browns of the trees and hills reflected off the shimmering silent water with dashes of green here and there along the shore. The high-pitched whistle of a shore bird broke the silence and highlighted the peace of the morn. A few gleaming little cottages nestled in among the trees and a cluster of worn-out old work buildings and sheds crouched at the foot of the old dock. A small, scruffy workboat lounged at its mooring, while *Free Spirit*, with her awning still at attention, rested at the end of the pier. A slight mist was on the perfectly mirrorlike water. The mountains and trees shimmered from the surface. We hauled in our lines and headed out to the fjord. I was taking some pictures of the idyllic scene when a fog bank rolled in and over the harbor exit. As we watched, it started to blow toward us like a living, breathing blanket and we were soon enveloped in pea soup. With no desire to navigate the tiny, narrow, rock-strewn fjords by radar, we decided to just sit and watch. We drifted around a small wooden perch, its arrow silently pointing the way. The land masses would occasionally drift in and out of view as the fog thinned and thickened at random. It was one of the most relaxing and peaceful scenes we had yet experienced. Tired of drifting, we motored in close to the land and dropped our small Danforth to wait out the fog. The cover lifted about nine so we hauled anchor and motored into the fjord. After we had passed our first thirty-meter-high bridge, the fog showed up again and Cindy, who had been afraid of the narrow, rock-strewn passages shown on the chart, begged to turn around and take the wide fjord. That would have meant a longer passage in heavier winds and bigger seas and I quietly persisted. As we approached, the fog bank began to lift and drift away. The rest of the morning was sunny and as crisply clear as a fall day should be. We continued in some of the most beautiful narrow small fjords of our trip.

CHAPTER 14

The Final Leg

The day dawned crisp and cold. The morning was delightful, the sun feeling marvelous even through the foul-weather gear. We were heavily dressed for winter. It was the seventh of September and we were motoring through outstandingly beautiful fjords, narrower ones we dared not try on the way down. Some are scarcely roomier than canals, mere twenty- to thirty-foot-wide passes between rocks, but all are easily navigable. Even those that appeared barely negotiable on the chart proved to be well marked with perches, and we had no trouble. The scenery changed constantly. Some was lush and richly verdant, some as barren as a moonscape.

That evening we slept in a pretty little harbor south of Florø. The windlass was its usual cranky self the next morning, but we managed to haul off and settled in for the last miles to Målöy. We kept the canopy up and it remained a blessing as rain fell intermittently.

In Målöy we contacted Gunnar and Evelyn and invited them over for barbecued steak while we finalized arrangements for the next day. We had originally planned to winter in Oslo and take further cruises in the Baltic the following year. The delayed start from the States had, of course, thrown off our schedule. But at least now our anxiety about the sea freezing so much farther north than Oslo was eased: We were told that freeze-ups seldom occur because Norwegian waters are bathed by the Gulf Stream.

We would not be at a wharf in our winter harbor, so we decided to offload our gear in Målöy. Gunnar lent us his car and we drove with a load of stuff to leave at the home of the man who would keep an eye on *Free Spirit* over the winter and repair her in the spring, the man I've called Edvard. Målöy's new and pleasant Hagen's Hotel allowed us to use their complex but effective commercial machines to do all our towels and other laundry. At first they refused to take any payment, but finally Cindy did persuade them to take a small token of our appreciation.

The following day we motored *Free Spirit* to the unnamed little harbor where we were to leave her for the winter. It was completely desolate, wooded, surrounded by mountains. Edvard's house stood on a cliff overlooking the harbor entrance. We stayed that night with him and his family and began to get to know these hospitable people better. They had built their huge, rambling home in sections. He had worked in the boatbuilding industry and thus knew several skilled workmen who were accustomed to working with fiberglass. Edvard allowed us to leave all our blankets, clothes, and canned goods, as well as electronic instruments, in his basement and attic. We finished off-loading the boat with his small workboat. The following day I winterized the engine, putting antifreeze in the radiator and in the cooling system. The pumps were pumped out with antifreeze, the head was filled with oil, and the water system was drained. We dropped and stored all sails and the dinghy engine.

Dinner that night with this warm, friendly family included delicious fish and an interesting local pudding for dessert. Saturday, Edvard's wife drove us to Målöy, and Saturday night Gunnar and Evelyn gave a dinner party for us, inviting several local friends. We stayed with them overnight and took the high-speed ferry to Bergen on Sunday afternoon.

Without *Free Spirit* we felt adrift. It was as if we had left a child alone. For the past three and a half months she had been our home and protector. She had introduced us to dozens of people we would never otherwise have met. She had shown us experiences we never had even dreamed possible. Even when planning for the trip, I had no clear idea of what would happen. Then places were just names; now they were living, dynamic entities. I had a logbook filled with all kinds of entries, from wind and sea states to shoreside sights and the addresses of new friends. Our camera had recorded thirty rolls of photographs. My eyes misted over with tears as we walked up to the door of our hotel. It was all over, and it had been everything I could have wished.

We immediately discerned that as hotel guests we were in a different ambience. The only people we met were the hotel staff, who were polite but formal. No one paid any attention to us. We felt, all of a sudden, like ordinary tourists rather than foreign adventurers. In sailing to Norway and along its coast, we had developed relationships with people in a meaningful way. To fly there and stay in a hotel would be to miss the whole experience we had shared. We took an early morning flight to London on Monday morning.

When we arrived at the customs desk at Logan Airport in Boston, the woman took one look at our yellow sailbags with the Norwegian stamps all over them and asked, "Did your three children come through here a couple of weeks ago?" We nodded, perplexed. What had our gang done now, I wondered. "Oh, yes." she said, "I recognize the seabags and the Norwegian stickers. Your kids were delightful and bubbly. They couldn't stop talking about all the wonderful things they had seen this summer. They were a pleasure to meet." She hurried us through, barely glancing at our bags.

Thus, we ended our transatlantic odyssey and Norwegian holiday. The drama of the adventure, the magnificence of the Norwegian mountain fjords and valleys, the generosity and spirit of her people, and the richness of her history will stay with us forever.

CHAPTER 15

Trials and Triumph

The winter passed on wings of exultation. Word of the success of our adventure spread quickly among friends and associates. Requests for speaking engagements came in from all over New England. Then, seemingly in the blink of an eye, I was back in Norway. Thrusting her bow bravely into the steep chop of the North Sea, *Free Spirit* again drew even with Stadlandet. The evil peninsula, reknowned for its bedevilment of ship and crew, was shrouded in mist. Sunlight danced on the seas and dazzled us with her bejeweled tapestry. No sails were yet bent on. Our departure had been hurried. The sailbags were tossed in a pile on the cabin floor. No sooner were we free of the lee than we were tossed like a cork in a maelstrom.

Peter and Phil quickly took to their bunks, victims of the sudden exposure to offshore conditions. It was left to me, the old man, to struggle with the 460-square-foot mainsail. Try as I would, however, I could not get enough of a purchase on it in the writhing, leaping cabin to thrust it into the cockpit. I reached for the storm trysail, a manageable bundle, and threw it from the companionway to the cockpit floor. Gradually easing my way forward on my belly, dragging the storm sail after me, I inched my way to the mast, hauled the head of the sail out of the bag, and began to work it onto the trysail track. With the sail finally set and drawing, I was able to heave to on an offshore tack as all hell broke loose from the heavens.

Odin, the sea god was speaking for his people. How dare I leave so precipitously? I knew the penalty for his wrath, but the risk of return was more of a reality than I dared face. How do you explain a friend gone mad with greed? How do you deal with a foreign legal system when you don't even know the language, never mind the rules? We had repairs done to our bow and foredeck for a price agreed upon in advance. One week prior to picking up the boat, with all bills paid, I learned that the agreed price wasn't good enough and the "friend" who'd watched over our boat all winter wanted an additional $8,000. Furthermore, to prevent us from leaving, he had secreted our sails and life raft—to ensure the payment of the ransom. But even with little hope of obtaining legal assistance despite written contracts to the contrary, I had managed to turn tragedy into triumph.

The previous fall and winter, while *Free Spirit* bobbed at anchor in her little Norwegian harbor, I had quickly and enthusiastically become reinvolved with my medical practice. The four months' leave of absence had totally reinvigorated my excitement and dedication. I enjoyed my patients, the nurses, the work, and even the responsibility. The summer's holiday had meant a total rebirth of my career.

Cindy returned to Xerox, but with the turmoil beginning in that industry, decided to take a new job as director of sales for a computer software company. The salary boost was something we both appreciated now. With major debt shaping up as a controlling factor on all our decisions for the next several years, every little bit helped. Peter had started his last year in high school and was beginning to sound out colleges. Elizabeth became immersed in her social life and casually returned to school. John was a sixth grader in the Wellesley Middle School.

I had six weeks vacation to take in 1983. Cindy arranged with her new employer for four weeks. Peter and I planned to bring *Free Spirit* across to England, and the rest of the family would join us on the Isle of Wight to enjoy Cowes Week. Further explorations of the west coast of Europe would take us south to Portugal, where we could leave the boat for the winter. Thereafter we could decide whether to explore the Mediterranean Sea or bring her back to the United States. Excitement began to brew in the Gould house as all of us looked forward to new adventures abroad. I had written Gunnar and Evelyn and they were looking forward to seeing us again. I also wrote to our friend Philippe, in Paris. We had, of course, met in Bergen. He invited us to stop in and visit at his summer house on the Brittany coast. It began to look as if this summer was going to be as brilliantly exciting as the last.

Since my time was more limited this year, I asked Peter to fly over two weeks ahead of me to help prepare the boat for the voyage. He arranged to have his school friend, Phil, join him. Phil would then sail with us from Norway to the Isle of Wight and would subsequently join his own family in Germany. Peter and Phil left for Norway in early July. Almost simultaneously with their departure, I began to get the first rumblings of trouble brewing over the price of *Free Spirit*'s repairs.

After some frustrating conversations with Norwegian friends and American bankers and lawyers, and an anxious call from Peter with more worrying details, I left Boston for Norway several days earlier than I'd planned. Flying into Bergen with only a small seabag, I arranged to charter a private seaplane for the last 200-mile trip to the isolated fjord that held my boat. I arrived at 10:30 P.M. on a Saturday (it was still light of course), and splashed down next to *Free Spirit* with a flourish, like James Bond.

Peter and Phil were delighted to see me. They had been treated well by Edvard and his family but were quite concerned with the developing events. With the obstruction from our avaricious hosts (the sails and life raft were who-knows-where), they had been able to do little. Now I took charge and set about readying the ship as best I could for the sea. The repairs were inspected and seemed to be nicely completed. I sent word that I wanted to meet my nemesis the next day to settle the claim. A fist-slamming confrontation ensued, in which he tried to *increase* the amount of extortion and I countered with a threat to sue for breach of contract. He backed down, shaken by my controlled fury, and even returned the missing sails and life raft. We hustled to the boat, tossed everything aboard, and headed out to sea.

We hove to as the rising storm blew in out of the south-west. I was sick myself now, and once I had secured the ship, I hurried below to collapse behind a lee cloth on one of the berths. I was exhausted from the long journey to reach this extreme of Norway, an all-night rush to prepare for sea, the settling of accounts, and the past six-hour struggle to secure *Free Spirit* in a rising gale. Exhaustion and fear lay on me like a wet blanket.

As luck would have it, we were driven north by the gale. It blew for three days with sustained winds of fifty knots and seas of twenty feet. But these were not the big, broad twenty-footers of the open ocean. These were like surf at the beach. The shallow waters of the North Sea caused the waves to break over us one after another, rolling over our decks from stern to stem. Day after day we were driven north. The temperature was only about forty degrees and we were cold as well as wet.

Occasionally, I rose from my berth to get liquids or nourishment and to feed my wretched crew. On the third day we heard a loud rumble from the forepeak and the boat turned sideways to the seas. The sixty-pound CQR anchor had broken its lashings, leapt off the bowsprit, crossed over the other anchor and dashed to the bottom of the sea. Two hundred feet of ⅜-inch chain went with it. We were now anchored on the sea bottom in a howling gale. I struggled with a halyard on a winch to try and haul the chain back onto its own roller and gypsy so that I could use the windlass to haul it up. The effort was singularly unsuccessful, and we ended up cutting the lashing for the chain in the locker and slipping the whole affair. We lost anchor, chain, and the spare genoa halyard on that fiasco. The seas were giants, reaching out to snatch us from the deck of our little ship. Several swirled around our waists, drawing us inexorably to the edges of disaster. Only our trusty Lirakis safety harnesses kept us tethered to the ship. We set the storm staysail, and with that drawing forward and the trysail driving aft, we began to sail due west across the path of the storm.

By next morning conditions had moderated and we were able to bend on and set full sail. We sailed south and west. Over the next several days, we slowly worked our way south past the Shetland Islands toward Scotland. The boys began to recover their spirits, and sunlight dappled the waters, seeming to laugh at our previous trials. I felt strangely incomplete. Part of my ship was gone and this always leaves me with a feeling of emptiness and vague unease until I can make her whole again. I was able to replace the chain in Scotland, but the CQR would have to await our arrival at the Isle of Wight in southern England.

Periodically, we spotted a black jumble of thrusting pipes and platforms, an oil rig looking for all the world like a gigantic erector set that someone had put together with all the pieces that came in the box, just so they would be used. At times, and from certain angles, they resembled some prehistoric monster stalking us behind the waves. At night, however, they were lit up like Christmas trees and threw a welcoming glow of humanity over the shifting seas.

As we approached the northern coast of Scotland, a large Danish sailing ship, one of the old square-riggers currently used as a sailing school, hove into view. We motorsailed over to get a closer look and wave to her crew. Laundry festooned her decks and I thought she must feel guilty at being caught thus in other than harbor trim.

As we approached the Scottish mainland we ran out of fuel in our main tanks. I switched to the auxiliary tank for the run to the harbor. In the haste of our departure, we had neglected to top our tanks. At last we motored wearily into the grimy commercial harbor welcoming us to Aberdeen, a strange, forbidding city with gray granite everywhere.

CHAPTER 16

Scottish Interlude

I now had to face needed repairs in Aberdeen. New anchor chain was a high priority. Tying up at a commercial quay, we put out all our fenders and fender boards. The docks were disgracefully dirty and oily. A slick of oil covered the harbor. Aberdeen, known for her large fishing fleet, university center, and surrounding castles, is now heavily involved in servicing the offshore oil fields. The city seemed entirely constructed of old, gray (and occasionally pink) granite rock. All the buildings, walls, and sidewalks used this universal medium, creating the impression of a great walled city. A collection of pubs within walking distance of the harbor were crowded and impersonal, lending little warmth or charm. Some were oriented toward a younger student population but did not attract my crew.

After arranging for help with the refrigeration, which needed a charge, I located a business that sold ⅜-inch galvanized chain and bought 200 feet. Since the plow anchor had gone to the bottom, I hauled out the reliable seventy-five-pound Herreshoff from the bottom of a sail locker and put her on deck. Problems with the stop sole-noid on my engine were corrected by an engineer on a British oil rig diving vessel docked in front of us. To thank him, I treated the engineer and his buddy to dinner that evening.

With our repairs behind us, we then spent a delightful day exploring the Scottish countryside. We hired a taxi and took a ride out to Balmoral Castle, the queen of England's summer palace. Built on the site of an earlier hunting lodge belonging to King Robert II of Scotland, Balmoral had been owned by Sir Robert Gordon. In the nineteenth century, rebuilt as a retreat for Queen Victoria, it was transformed into a magnificent white granite baronial palace, surrounded by manicured lawns, hedges, and gardens. It features a large ballroom and a square tower topped by a round turret; the whole rises against a splendid backdrop of wooded hills and mountains. The superb grounds and peaceful walks were a pleasant contrast to our recent donnybrook with the North Sea. The River Dee bubbled nearby through a valley richly cloaked in forest. The Scottish towns through which we passed were fresh and clean; the mica in their granite buildings sparkled in the sun. After a day spent sightseeing in the environs of Balmoral and Aberdeen, we collapsed in our bunks at midnight.

After refueling, we set our sights for the English Channel, motoring out of Aberdeen harbor at noontime on a Tuesday. On Saturday we were due to rendezvous with Cindy and the other children at Cowes on the Isle of Wight, about 550 miles away.

We set off on a cool, breezy, partly cloudy day for the middle and lower reaches of the North Sea. Our plan was to sail far enough off the coast to stay away from the shoals and flats that threaten all vessels near the English shore.

The passage was marked by the failure of our autopilot. The Neco pilot had performed yeoman's service in our previous adventures, and was sorely missed on this trip. We steered by hand, day and night. The nights were quite chilly and often tinged with fog. As we approached the southern reaches of the Straits of Dover, more and more shipping crowded the channel. The cargo of many nations was converging on one of the world's busiest waterways. Shipping was kept to strict lanes and a sharp eye was needed to avoid collision.

Finally, we turned the southeast tip of England at Dungeness and made for the Isle of Wight. The big radome at the Nab, emitting its radar signals in waves, allowed us to focus in on this tower at sea and led us into the solent between the Isle of Wight and the mainland. We pulled into Cowes late in the evening to find every possible dock space and anchorage spoken for by the fleet attending Cowes Week. We approached a very luxurious eighty-foot American maxiracer and their crew most reluctantly took our lines. We quickly turned in for some sleep, but later that evening the wind rose, seas built, and we were forced to leave our refuge to tie to a large buoy in the center of the ferry turnaround. The next morning we were able to get our own dockspace well up the River Medina.

CHAPTER 17

Cowes to Port Manech

*N*ow, at last, with 1100 miles of storm-tossed passages behind us, we could look forward to the beginning of an enjoyable vacation. We had just returned to the ship from a quick shopping expedition to find Cindy, Elizabeth, and John tucking their bags away. Squeals of welcome and hugs and kisses all around alternated with a barrage of questions about our trip, the confrontation in Norway, and how we were able to get away from *Free Spirit*'s captors. Phil left the next day to join his family on a trip to Germany.

Gradually, we settled in and began to explore Cowes. The town, divided in half by the River Medina, was in a holiday mood. Loaded with tourists and sailors, townsfolk and hawkers, it was a gaudy scene. Dozens of little shops and restaurants and pubs competed for our attention— and we tried them all. My favorite was the small studio run by Bekin of Cowes, the well-known marine photographer. The history of his shop, started by his father, is a history of the development of photography. I met the grand man himself and spent a delightful time tossing off sea stories back and forth with him.

I also took the opportunity to stop in at the Ratsey sail loft. This had been the starting point, eighty years earlier, for my friend, the sailmaker Colin Ratsey, who had made most of our sails. Several of the Ratsey family were happy to hear about their cousin now off in America.

After three days of sightseeing, pub-hopping, and people-watching, Peter and I took the ferry to Portsmouth, where a large ship's chandlery was able to sell us a seventy-five-pound CQR plow anchor to replace the one we'd left on the bottom of the North Sea. Our SatNav was not working, and of course the autopilot had failed just after we left Aberdeen. We found an electronics specialist who was able to repair our autopilot but could not fix the SatNav.

We stayed a week in Cowes, then cast off, rounded the Needles, and set a course for Concarneau on the Brittany coast. Our course would take us near the Channel Islands through passages with fierce tides and currents, around the Ile d'Ouessant (Ushant), and into the Bay of Biscay. We were navigating simply with compass and watch. Our Loran was getting few readings, our SatNav was on the blink, and the weather was cloudy, with twenty-five- to thirty-knot winds giving a bumpy and fractious ride. Fortunately, as we approached the Ushant, a large radome was clearly visible at twenty miles on our radar and guided us past some otherwise invisible shoals. The weather cleared as we entered the Bay of Biscay and bright sunshine greeted us as we approached Concarneau.

The entry to Concarneau led through long, sunlit shallows with marks showing the way. A shallow bar protected the entrance to the river, but we slipped over with room to spare at high noon. Sprinkled over the wide bay of the river mouth were a flock of commercial fishing boats, small freighters, and a gaggle of pleasure boats of all sizes and types. As we neared Concarneau itself, we could see the old town and a gathering of modern office buildings. A long cement pier shielded the town's inner harbor from the river traffic and was lined with numerous commercial craft. Within, we could see sailboat masts clustered and we poked our bow through the narrow entry. The wind was blowing briskly on our starboard quarter. Hundreds of pleasure craft hung from dozens of finger piers off our starboard bow; not an empty slip could be seen. To our left the little harbor opened up into a small bight with commercial docks and more pleasure boat piers. I decided to commit us to this path and quickly swung the wheel over to enter the bight. The wind blew us quickly into the little harbor, but again I could see no open slip available. As I hugged the left-hand pier, I saw that we were going to have trouble turning in the little basin. I swung the wheel hard over to starboard and gave the engine a little burst of power to bring the bow around. *Free Spirit* slowly swung her eighteen tons and we headed straight for a large schooner tied to its pier. I hoped in vain that we would make the turn, but as we began to head into the wind, I could feel its strength increase, and it caught our bow and slowed the turn. As we neared catastrophe, I throttled back and thrust her into reverse. Dozens of nearby figures hurried to protect their boats with fenders and boathooks, but it looked as if we would come in broadside against half a dozen large sailboats. I swung the wheel hard over and gave the engine a strong thrust of the throttle. Fortunately, her clockwise-spinning prop tends to back more easily to the left, so I was able to get the bow into the eye of the wind. With inches to spare, I jammed her back into forward, threw the wheel hard over to starboard, and we managed to make the turn and head back toward the entrance.

In the meantime, shouts of concern turned to encouragement, and a few cheers met our efforts. Figures from the other side of the harbor began to beckon to us. I followed the gestures and waves, slipped into a narrow way between two finger piers, and found a little vacant slip awaiting us. It was impossible to actually make the turn, but willing hands took our lines and helped to guide us into the slip. With a tremendous feeling of relief, we settled in and secured our lines.

This was an entirely new experience for us. The town of Concarneau was a bustling, energetic continental little city with an authentic old town, walled off from the modern city and set on an island. This, the fortified Ville Clos, is connected to the town by a bridge that once was a drawbridge. In this medieval bastion we were quickly plunged into the milieu of the Middle Ages. Roses and flowers climbed all over the walls of the old town, giving it a festive air. We took photographs, poked our noses into every nook and cranny, and delighted in the open butcher shops and bakeries, the little taverns, and tiny cobblestone streets.

A phone call put me in touch with Philippe, whom we had met in Bergen harbor the previous summer. The next day Chantelle drove over to pick us up and guide us into the tricky entrance to Port Manech and the River Aven. Little Port Manech also had a shallow bar guarding its entrance, but with Chantelle's help, we easily found our way through the tortuous channel and came to lie at a mooring in front of Philippe's grand summer home. Philippe had given us his mooring, moving his own yacht 120 feet upriver. He, Joel, Chantelle, and Alan welcomed us warmly. They had a fine dinner for us that evening and we spent hours marveling at the fabulous pictures they had taken on their cruise to Spitsbergen the previous year. Scenes of icebergs, snow-capped mountains, and polar bears all right off the bow or stern of their yacht made for a dramatic photo session.

The following morning, we were driven around the countryside to see Bretagne, and then took a long dinghy ride up the river to Port Aven, where there was a traditional festival. The town is filled with art galleries and restaurants. Gaugin did much of his work here before fleeing for the pleasures of Tahiti. The food was delicious, the parades and traditional costumes a treat, and the street entertainers delightful. Light and tasty crêpes smothered in cream and berries made a smashing lunch. The Bretons were demonstrative in parading their special traditions, flag, and a pride in their own uniqueness.

A party was held in our honor at Philippe's and that evening Joel prepared a delicious dinner for us. By profession he is an attorney, but by temperament he is a fine chef, and aboard Philippe's yacht, he is the cook. We traced our adventures since we had last seen them and told them of our rather sketchy plans for the winter. They recommended Vilamoura in Portugal as a good place to leave *Free Spirit* unattended during the winter.

With approximately 600 miles to go and only two and a half weeks left, we departed the following morning, headed for Cape Finisterre. Everyone came to see us off and we traded addresses, as several of the young people expressed interest in doing the Atlantic crossing with me the next year.

CHAPTER 18

Spain and Portugal

*T*he first twelve hours of sailing we enjoyed sunny skies with an easy reaching breeze. At nightfall, we assigned watches and watched the barometer take a slow, steady dive. By morning, it was raining and we slogged on in foul-weather gear. Without SatNav or Loran, and in lowered visibility, we ran under dead reckoning. We had no current tables or tide tables. After forty-eight hours, with ever-thickening fog and rain, I began to worry that we might miss Cape Finisterre and find ourselves well out into the Atlantic without realizing it. We hoped to stop in Bayona to get a brief taste of Spain before heading on to Portugal.

Peering ahead while on watches, we could see very little except the six- to ten-foot seas. The radar showed no other shipping and little except rain squalls. Elizabeth called me below to see a particularly large squall on the radar. I took one look and said, "That's no squall, that's a mountain." We carefully picked our way toward the towering cliff, keeping our eyes peeled, and then suddenly, out of the mist, a huge mountainside, black in the dusk, rose in front of us. Combers crashed on the distant shore perhaps half a mile ahead of us. We eased off to run due west.

We sailed on through the night and into the next day before finally rounding Cabo de Finisterre. We had been pushed east at least sixty miles by a strong current in the bay. Rounding the big cape, we worked our way south to the entrance to Bayona and eased our way into the capacious harbor.

Bayona, typically Spanish in appearance, is a bustling town with few modern architectural adornments. Life seems rooted in the turn of the last century. A bustling marina hugs its southern shore, and the long line of wharfs and piers stretches well out into the harbor. The people left us to ourselves. Our eight o'clock dinner hour found us standing in a restaurant and watching the hired help eat. We quickly learned that restaurants never started serving until ten, and Spaniards prefer to eat at about eleven. This we never quite got used to. The kids found a large discotheque, however, and made friends with local young people. We had a hard time dragging John away from the bumper cars at a small amusement park near the marina. We talked with some other cruisers but found few who spoke English well. After two days we dropped our lines and headed for Lisbon.

The long passage down the Spanish and Portuguese coasts to Lisbon was marked by the lack of suitable harbors for a vessel like ours. After two days at sea we pulled into the outer harbor of Cascais, the resort town that guards the entry to the long commercial roads of the Tagus River leading to Lisbon proper. We were warned that Lisbon itself offers little in the way of hospitality to the pleasure yacht and were advised to stay where we were, anchored in thirty feet of water. The yacht club in Cascais allowed us to tie our dinghy to their docks so we could stretch our legs in the little town's square. Actually, this is quite a busy and prosperous place. Many wealthy Lisbonites have created a sort of suburban elegance with their villas in the surrounding hills. Cascais itself is quite old, with winding streets and fascinating old buildings. We walked and shopped and poked and stared to our hearts' content. The beach in town was busy on the weekend; we happily joined the crush.

On the third day, we caught the train for the thirty-mile ride into Lisbon. Built on seven hills in a series of terraces, Lisbon overlooks the Tagus, almost dwarfing its magnificence. The Alfama, old Roman and Moorish Lisbon, has narrow, winding, damp streets with steep twisting steps, arches, and ancient buildings with iron grilles and latticed balconies. Lisbon, with its numerous fountains, impressive modern buildings, statues, and gardens, would compare favorably with any city in the world. Towers, museums, and magnificent cathedrals drew us in.

After a very full day in Lisbon, we took the train back to Cascais and slept well in the peace of our little cabin on *Free Spirit*. With a week of such activities under our belts, we saw Peter off on a plane back to Boston so he could prepare for school.

We had made friends with the crew aboard a nearby fifty-two-foot schooner designed by Sparkman & Stephens. A beautiful vessel, she was was due to sail the next day for Gibraltar. We planned to sail with them as we were headed for the large marina at Vilamoura on the southern Portuguese coast. We hauled anchor together at ten in the morning and quickly discovered that ours was snagged on an obstruction on the bottom. They waved good-bye as we struggled with our gear. Two hours later we managed to free ourselves and set off in pursuit. It was a glorious sunny day with broad, white, puffy cumulus clouds. The wind was blowing strongly out of the north at twenty-five to thirty knots. The seas quickly built to nine or ten feet so we set the twin running sails for our trip down the coast. At 8:30 P.M. we spotted our friends in their schooner under a modest-sized spinnaker. Doing close to nine knots, we surfed by them. That night we watched carefully as we paralleled the coast. We were anxious not to miss the turn of the coastline, but found it difficult to follow either by sight or by radar because it was all low beach. We also didn't want to run aground. We kept three to five miles off, but found it nerve-racking trying to keep track of our position. At last we turned the coast early the next morning, and beat our way up to the entrance to Vilamoura.

The artificial jetty guarding the entry reached out in welcome to us and we pulled into the main dock. Customs formalities followed, and we were able to make arrangements to leave *Free Spirit* for the next several months. The marina was huge, with room for approximately a thousand boats. Assigned to a slip, we proceeded to secure our ship carefully for the gales sure to follow in the autumn. Then we began to explore the expensive boutiques and shops surrounding the marina. The food was good but expensive, and the marina was quite obviously an oasis of wealth on an extravagant and overbuilt section of the coast surrounded by utter poverty in the interior villages.

One day I was down below changing the engine oil and filters when Cindy cheerfully came aboard carrying a basket of laundry. She announced that she had met an American in the laundromat and thought that he sounded rather interesting. He apparently was quite well known, having published articles on several long cruises in the popular sailing magazines. I asked his name but she couldn't remember it. She said that he had sailed a little eighteen-foot boat around the world. "You don't mean Webb Chiles?" I exclaimed. "Yes, that's it!" she said. I asked her to bring him over and we invited him aboard to talk sailing. He proved to be as interesting and pleasant in person as are his writings. We had long conversations about our experiences. Cindy complained about all the bad weather on our passages. Webb responded that he had spent several years at sea, sailed around the world twice, and could only remember four or five perfect days in all his time at sea! This was a fortunate turn of events for us. The marina did not have the personnel to check the boat regularly for me. I was uncomfortable leaving her totally unsupervised over the winter. Webb offered to check her once a week and pump the bilge. This made me feel a lot better about leaving her.

Over the next three days, we met and developed a friendship with the crew of a large motor yacht next door. The owners, a South African yachtsman, his wife, and three children had pulled up stakes and quit the country, leaving a vast estate and a large business, because of their concern about the political situation there. They were headed to England for a new start in life. John quickly became friends with their young son, Wade. Several other young people began to turn up, and the dinghy again became an important social vehicle. John, Wade, and a young Canadian lad with the historical name John Paul Jones spent hours exploring cliffs and underwater sights. Using Wade's powerful little whaler as a water taxi they ferried cruisers to their yachts in the outer roadstead. The South African family's elder daughter tried to teach me how to windsurf. I tried and tried, but couldn't stay up in the gusty winds outside the harbor. The beaches outside the harbor were long and beautiful—and topless. It was a new and very different experience for us.

Gradually, we got ourselves packed and organized to fly back to Boston. Both Cindy and I had to return to work, and John and Elizabeth needed to start school. After another summer of exciting and dramatic adventures, *Free Spirit* would lie in Portugal awaiting my return.

CHAPTER 19

Southwest in the Trades

*W*hen we left, Portugal, *Free Spirit* was sitting quietly next to her dock, festooned with docking lines, chafing gear, and fenders. Every bit of movable gear had been stowed below and she was locked up tight. The weather was still beautiful and hot, but the winter would be cold, raw, and full of frequent storms. The boat looked small and lonely as the taxi drove us off to the airport.

After we arrived in Boston, I began to have second thoughts. I hated having my boat across an ocean with no assurance that she would be all right in my absence. My past experiences had not encouraged me to trust boatyards in foreign countries; I had little recourse if anything got out of hand. Furthermore, I now preferred to take care of many of the little jobs myself, and this was only possible if the boat was at home under my care.

Ultimately I decided to forgo further European travels until I could commit to taking at least a year off. I therefore began a quest to find crew to help me bring *Free Spirit* back to this hemisphere. I planned to sail to the Canary Islands, stop for a brief visit, and then bring her to the Caribbean.

A study of charts of the area, and Don Street's writings, convinced me that Antigua would be an ideal place to aim for. Street's description of Antigua as a place with a friendly local population and many varied and protected anchorages, including English Harbour, proved to be something of an overstatement. However, I would find this out much later.

I contacted the Cruising Club of America and advertised in local sailing magazines since my own family would be unable to take time off to crew for me. I hoped to bring the boat across in the trade wind season (usually starting in December and petering out in April). Slowly names began to come in, phone calls were made, and a crew list began to evolve. We finally chose four (I've changed their names). Two were young men in their early twenties: Steve, with enthusiastic but limited coastal experience, and Dave, with much more extensive experience and time spent on a seagoing sail-training vessel as well as a family yacht. Doug owned his own midsize sailboat; and Ted had retired at an early age from his own business, was an airplane pilot, and had chartered a number of yachts in southern waters.

We met to discuss the practicalities, what each was responsible for (mainly his own clothes and gear, and plane tickets), and I tried to assess each one's suitability for the trip. This would be the first time that I would be sailing with complete strangers, and I wanted to be sure that it would work out. Despite the effort made, personal interviews, and conversations with references, the mix did not work out as well as I had hoped. In fact, the experience convinced me that I would prefer to sail single-handed rather than subject myself to a long voyage with strangers again.

In late October, I took a long weekend to fly to Portugal to check on the boat. After an arduous journey I reached *Free Spirit* late in the afternoon. She was sitting quietly at her pier, just as I'd left her. Her chafing gear was a little frayed, but the lines were relatively unscathed. Her bilges were dry and I sought out Webb, who described some of the nasty storms that had visited the region during my absence. I dined with my South African friends, still in harbor, and later charged *Free Spirit*'s batteries and turned over the engine. A day later, I found myself winging my way back across the Atlantic.

In the course of my planning for the coming voyage, I decided to precook and freeze a number of meals at home because of the difficulty of getting quality meats in Portugal. We would each carry frozen pork roast, barbecued chicken, or steaks in special freezer packs stuffed in our luggage for the long trip to Portugal and down to the boat.

It was the sixteenth of January when we gathered at Logan Airport and crossed the broad expanse of Ocean to Lisbon. We rented a car in Lisbon and headed down to Vilamoura. The countryside was hilly and dry with scrub brush for vegetation and none of the green beauty of a New England scene. As we approached the artificial landscaping of the Algarve coast, condominium high-rise apartments and hotels greeted us, and soon we were at the entrance gates of the Vilamoura marina. We did some more shopping in the local supermarkets to fill out our supplies for the crossing, though the choice of vegetables and canned goods was limited. After clearing up my account at the marina, we slipped our lines at 3:22 P.M. on January 18, 1984. We said our good-byes to Webb who, with his friend Jill, took pictures of us as we waved adieu.

Everything seemed shipshape for the crossing. At this

point the crew was helpful and knowledgeable and they were able to take over much of the handling of the ship, freeing me for the chores of navigation. By six we were flying under full sail with a full moon rising off our port quarter. It felt glorious to be back on *Free Spirit*. She rose to the gentle swells with ease. The stuffing gland around the propeller shaft began to leak and I tightened this with the appropriate wrench. With the repaired SatNav programmed and the *Grand Canyon Suite* on the stereo, we were all at peace.

That night we helped Ted celebrate his birthday with a candle in a big round loaf of Portuguese bread we served with our spaghetti dinner. With careful watch-keeping, we altered course to go astern of two large ships heading for the Mediterranean Sea. At that point the crew seemed first-rate. They knew just what to do without being told.

The following day was lovely, albeit cool. We had a relaxed day of reading while close reaching at seven knots under the genoa and mainsail. Conditions remained easy. It was cool, dry, crisp, and clear.

On January twentieth, we continued to move south in delightful conditions, tacking off somewhat to the east because we could not hold our course directly. It remained cool and crisp but felt pleasant if one wore a sweater and a jacket.

The wind varied from light motoring conditions to gusty, twenty-knot winds on our nose. By 1500 hours, all was peaceful. Steve was on watch, Dave was writing, and Ted and I were reading. Doug was asleep. That night, under a full moon with lots of stars, we passed another ship fairly close by. We had brought a weatherfax to see if it would aid us in finding the trades and avoiding nasty weather; it gave us some trouble but we finally got it working.

On January twenty-second, our fourth day out, we had cloudy conditions and were on a run under the twins. It was rather rolly and we kept a reefed main up and strapped in to steady her. This was eventually changed to the trysail, which could handle the roll better. Skies cleared that evening and it was indeed a beautiful sky. We calculated that we were seventy-three miles north of Tenerife, in the Canaries, where we planned to stop to reprovision. By the next morning, several things needed repair. The batteries were not charging properly, the battery condition indicator switch had broken, and water was influxing through the shower drain. We closed the seacock to the drain, repaired the indicator switch, and recharged the batteries. At six-thirty in the morning, the halyard to the twins parted due to chafe at the radar bracket. We put the running sails back up on the spare genoa halyard.

We arrived in Tenerife that afternoon. A search of the main harbor revealed no facilities for yachts. Locals directed us up the coast to a small harbor used by fishing boats and a few yachties. We asked for customs and no one seemed to know anything about it. After a two-hour search, we decided to break all the rules and took a bus into town to do some shopping. We spent half the night there and had a ball. I bought a locally made guitar of very good quality at a reasonable price. Food was also of pretty good quality and we stocked up as best we could.

The next day we were again off. As we worked our way south to find the trades, we began to have our first major troubles. On the twenty-eighth of January I raised the genoa to increase boat speed off the wind. The staysail was also set. The boat spun off a big sea and the mainsail came aback and split at one of the seams. We furled it and set the twins. Unfortunately, with the twins on the spare genoa halyard, they could not be set properly because the halyard pulled from the wrong angle, and they furled imperfectly. The whisker pole fittings for both poles broke within fifteen minutes of each other and one of the poles bent seriously with the strength of the wind. We took the bent pole down and finally had to take down the whole rig. The staysail went back up after six hours of struggle.

We were now sailing in the trades, but they were not the trade winds of my dreams. We had a minigale blowing at least thirty knots with higher gusts from the southeast. Boarding seas now soaked us at the most unexpected times.

The next day we sustained more damage. The genoa started to split at a seam. We took it down and began a series of sail repairs. After we got the mainsail repaired and back up, I tried an intentional jibe, but did it badly. The mainsheet caught the binnacle and tore the compass off. It looked like a head rolling on the cockpit floor. We managed to repair it and replaced it, rewiring the light. Then, the coup de grace—the autopilot stopped working. We were about two hundred miles off the coast of Africa at the time. The prospect of steering the remaining two thousand miles by hand had little appeal, and neither did the thought of fighting our way back against those boisterous trades. I took the autopilot control head out of the cockpit and into the cabin. As the seas tossed our boat to and fro, I took it apart to see if one of the boarding seas had soaked its interior. It appeared dry, but I kept it in a warm oven overnight to see if this would help. We hand-steered all night and the next day I reinstalled the control head. No luck. It still wouldn't work.

I crawled into the starboard sail locker to see what else might have gone wrong. It is terribly frustrating to be at sea with complex electronic gear that one depends on com-

pletely and have it break down. I spent the morning in the
bilge studying the workings of my autopilot. I finally found
that a pin that connected the drive shaft to the chain drive
had sheared off. It was nowhere to be seen in the bilge. I
replaced it with a stainless bolt, which worked until eleven
that night when it too broke. I now tried a fastpin (a solid,
stainless fitting I had aboard) but this lasted only twenty
minutes before it cracked and split in half. The crew steered
by hand all night. I was up at seven in the morning and
finished repairing the genoa. I then tackled the autopilot
again. It was apparently of utmost importance to center
the autopilot once I got a pin back in. Otherwise, it would
force itself against one of the stops and break any pin.

I studied the instruction booklet. Essentially, it described
heading the boat in a north/south direction, tying up at a
dock in quiet conditions, and centering the rudder by direct vision. We were of course sailing in twenty-foot seas
with thirty-knot winds in a westerly direction. There was
no way that we were about to change our course to be
beam on to those seas. After several false starts, we finally
got a pin that looked as if it wouldn't break. I drilled out
both ends of a fastpin with a hand drill, Doug hardened
it over the propane stove, and we wired it into position.
In the meantime Dave was on the wheel as I called out
course changes to him (I was able to estimate rudder position from within the bilge). After another three hours of
adjustments, we had it repaired. We sailed under cloudy
skies with the seas cresting to about fifteen to twenty feet.
Squirreled away in the cockpit locker for much of the day,
I couldn't have cared less about the lack of sunshine. The
repairs made that day have lasted the six years since and
still function perfectly. By February second after a pleasant
interlude of two sunny days, it started to blow again. We

shortened sail and ran wing and wing under deeply reefed main and with the staysail hauled out to the end of a whisker pole. We rode fast and hard. With the wind strengthening, we battened down everything below. After an evening of heavy squalls, we finally settled into a rolling, oily calm. This lasted for about seven hours, and soon we were again bowling along in the trades.

As the days passed, the crew became more and more touchy. I also found that my nerves were on edge. No longer did we work together smoothly. I would request a course change to allow us to take the seas on our quarter and Doug would insist that this was the wrong thing to do. He preferred the rhumb line course on one bearing in spite of the heavy rolling that a direct downwind run gave us. I had to insist on doing things my way as captain of the ship and found it annoying to be forced to pull rank in this manner.

The next problem was Doug's raiding of the freezer. I had saved ice cream for a special treat about halfway across. Doug pulled it out without asking and was well into it when I caught him. I forced him to put it back, and when he started to resist, I blew up at him.

Ted grew grouchier and grouchier too. I baked bread most mornings, but our little oven would not hold more than two small loaves. We consumed both loaves for breakfast and lunch, and when dinner rolled around, I had no bread to serve. We had also run out of vegetables. Two weeks at sea and they were all gone. We had a dinner of pork roast and rice, with a special gravy. I was able to serve some canned peaches for dessert. Ted griped that we had no bread or vegetables with the meal. I found that I could not deal with this as easily as I ordinarily might have. I seemed to have lost my sense of humor, and I complained bitterly that my culinary efforts were not appreciated. Since I not only did all the cooking and meal planning but the navigation, repairs, and some of the sailing and watch-keeping as well, I was particularly sensitive.

Each of us was increasingly isolated and resentful of the others. The two boys remained pleasant but aloof, and the three of us older men developed a smoldering mutual hostility. As we neared our destination, I found that I was only comfortable when I was standing up. Every spot on my body was sore and bruised due to the constant rolling of the boat. The other crew must have felt the same, but we each kept our feelings to ourselves.

Two days out of Antigua, a hose broke, emptying water out of our two remaining water tanks into the bilge. We were out of fresh water. Fortunately, we had plenty of soda and juices aboard so that we were not about to die of thirst. The new development made Doug absolutely panicked with fear, however, and he couldn't be reasoned with. This was especially acute for him because he innately distrusted my celestial navigation. He did not truly believe that we would arrive on schedule in Antigua.

The stars at night were magnificent as we approached the Caribbean. Dave and I spent two nights trying to iden-tify constellations and taking evening star sights. The SatNav, which had been repaired that fall, had been nonfunctional for the last thousand miles. Celestial sights became of par-amount importance. This, of course, demonstrates why a ship's captain should never rely solely on electronic nav-igational tools.

We found Antigua within fifteen minutes of my esti-mated time of arrival. Dave spotted land first. We passed south of the island, finally pulling into English Harbour late in the afternoon of February fourteenth. The last week had been so traumatic that the crew simply disappeared as soon as we cleared customs and we haven't seen each other since. The difficulties of living together with strangers for an extended period in close quarters with increasingly uncomfortable conditions left its mark, and made me appreciate the value of having my own family as crew.

I spent the several days arranging for someone to take care of *Free Spirit* in English Harbour. Labor was cheaper there than in the States, so I hired a local workman to take the teak down to bare wood and bring it back to its usual glow. Other yachtsmen told of rampant thievery and break-ins on the island and in the harbor. By arranging for someone to work on the boat, I hoped that we would somehow be spared. The poverty of the Antiguan people was very disconcerting. They frequently badgered the wealthier yachtsmen for handouts or pressed for use of their services for all sorts of odd jobs or taxi rides. The island was dry and unappealing except for the few spots that had been developed by wealthy commercial interests.

Cindy, John, and Elizabeth flew in and we all began to unwind. John developed abdominal pain on the trip down and immediately we had to consider whether or not he should be flown back to Boston. The local hospital was in a hovel and as a physician I would never have allowed John to receive emergency surgery there. I took him down to the boat and examined him. He was complaining of upper abdominal pain and had tenderness in the upper abdomen but none in the lower. The pain had now persisted for four hours. I decided that it was likely that he had a peptic ulcer that was eroding away his intestinal wall. Fortunately, *Free Spirit* is admirably equipped with a complete medication locker and I started him on Tagamet and antacids. Tagamet was relatively new at the time and would prove itself capable of almost eliminating the need for peptic ulcer surgery. John's symptoms gradually subsided over the next twenty-four hours but I kept him on a bland diet for several days. John Paul, one of the young friends he made in Portugal, had sailed into English Harbour with his family the previous week. He was very adept at quickly learning all there was to know about his surroundings. He brought John up to date on the English Harbour attractions, kept him company, and together they went on numerous dinghy trips and explorations. John, as always, sick or no, has been able to find friends wherever he went. No other young person I know has so many close friends, or is as capable of meeting and befriending people in all classes of society—even when he can't speak their language.

Snorkeling at the end of the harbor and in a nearby bay was fascinating, and great exercise. I have always loved to swim and this offered a good excuse to do so. We beached and partied and sailed to a number of little coves. The navigation was tricky, however, the waters poorly marked, and many of the interesting harbors mentioned by Don Street had entrances that kept me tense as we negotiated our passage. We spent a pleasant ten days in Antigua and then flew back to the States, leaving *Free Spirit* bobbing at anchor in a protected corner of the harbor.

CHAPTER 20

Closing the Circle

*R*elief, sadness, fatigue—which of these was uppermost? I'm not sure. All played a role in my thinking at the time. I was immensely relieved that I had been able to get the boat out of Europe and closer to home. Not only was it impossible to take care of *Free Spirit* properly when she was so far away, it was also very difficult to afford the bank payments during the high interest rate period of the early 1980s. I would have considered selling her in Europe, but the extremely high value of the dollar at that time made such a purchase impractical for European buyers. I had to bring her home either to sell or take care of.

Now she was in the Caribbean and again out of my control. The local man responsible for her care had been well spoken for by a local sailmaker, but essentially he was an unknown quantity to me, and represented a risk. Boat robberies were at a peak in Antigua and *Free Spirit* was a major unprotected potential target.

I began to prepare for the last link in the circle. I decided to take her to Chesapeake Bay, where there was a large and active sailboat market where I might be able to sell her. The previous month's crossing from Portugal had taught me the risks in being at sea with strangers. All the crew had been competent sailors, but disagreements outweighed any advantages of the extra help. I didn't need to be second-guessed on the correctness of each decision. I didn't need to have complaints about the food. Most of all, I found it onerous to have to plan for, cook for, and be responsible for a number of strangers. It would be easier to care for myself. Cooking for one, cleaning up for one, and having no one to answer to seemed to make the most sense. Finally, I had always wanted to make a long single-handed passage. It was one of the few challenges left to me. I had made several coastal passages alone, but none far at sea.

During my preparations, a good friend of many years asked about my planned final voyage in *Free Spirit*. A fifty-five-year-old peer he was my landlord at the office. He expressed interest in the trip. I told him that he could come if he wanted to, never dreaming that he would actually do so. He didn't really seem to be a risk-taker—and a short-handed 1750-mile passage was definitely a risk.

He finally decided to do it, and I acquiesced. Bob was certainly not a stranger. I had known him for fifteen years and knew that he was easy to get along with. Still, I had not lived with him, and I was acutely aware that there might be problems. As it turned out, he was excellent company and although his complete lack of experience as a sailor meant that he would not feel safe out of the cockpit (on deck) at sea, his ability to be at peace in even the most extreme circumstances created an atmosphere of relaxation and humor under otherwise tense conditions.

I flew into Antigua at the end of April, 1984. *Free Spirit* was lying peacefully at her anchor. The local man had done a good job with her teak, and she sparkled in the sun. Her bottom, however, was festooned with a collection of barnacles. I had chosen not to have her hauled until I returned to the States because Antigua slipway was relatively expensive. Additionally, she had been painted the previous June in Norway and I ordinarily only haul out once a year.

I had not counted on the extraordinary growth of marine organisms in a tropical environment. Long strands of goose barnacles hung from her rudder. Thick encrustations enveloped all her undersides. I had arrived on the weekend and I had just a few days to clear her, load up on supplies, and prepare for the voyage. A couple of youngsters were willing to help. I donned a mask, tank, regulator, and fins and slipped overboard on Monday morning. Armed with a three-inch scraper I attacked the marine hordes. As I worked on the deeper parts, the youngsters attacked the waterline. Within an hour or so, we had her reasonably clean. As I broke the surface, out of air in my tank, I began to itch all over. Little stinging shrimp were attached to my skin and the exposure to air seemed to make their stings explode. I writhed within my own skin and dove into the shower to try and rid myself of the torture.

Fifteen minutes later I was toweled dry, powdered, dressed in shorts and sitting in the cockpit with a cool beer. An antihistamine was settling down the itching and I was beginning to feel satisfaction. The boat looked good, I was ready for the trip, and all should be fine. Bob was due to arrive on Thursday and we planned to leave as soon as he flew in.

That evening, I had dinner with Webb Chiles and a friend of his from another boat. Webb had crossed from Portugal in late February under similar conditions to those

I had experienced a month earlier. I recounted the difficulties of crossing an ocean with a group of strangers. When I described Ted's outraged complaint that we had run out of fresh bread and vegetables, they roared with laughter. The pork roast and rice I had served seemed to my audience to be the ultimate in transoceanic luxury. They were accustomed to ocean crossings with canned spam and Dinty Moore beef stew. Webb indicated that similar experiences had led him to prefer solo sailing.

I arranged to clear customs, Bob arrived as planned on May third, and we set out about noon. Bob had never been aboard a sailboat before and was intrigued with all the gadgets and winches, the navigational gear, and the living arrangements. He piloted his own plane and, on one occasion, had flown with his wife, Peggy, up to Alaska. He was therefore familiar with the principles of navigation. I explained what our course of action was and he seemed pleased.

I planned to sail out of the Caribbean into the Atlantic in order to clear most of the islands. This would give us rougher conditions but would allow us to sail long distances without having to watch constantly for ship traffic or concern ourselves with running into a reef at night. We had fourteen days to bring our ship into the Chesapeake and then were due back at work.

Two hours out of Antigua and I was feeling seasick. I had taken no Stügeron, the conditions were bouncy with six- to eight-foot seas, and we were on a close reach. Bob seemed to be unaffected. Under autopilot we drove through the seas. Four hours later I tried to start the engine and found that it would not work. A leak somewhere in the fuel system was bringing air into the fuel, so she had an air lock. With Bob's help on the start button I bled her and we got her started.

That evening we ran out of propane. There had been no place convenient to English Harbour to obtain a refill and I had no gauges aboard the boat to indicate the state of our tanks. For the remainder of the trip, we either ate cold meals or prepared dishes on the heat of the engine. This led to some interesting experiments. I learned that one can cook many dishes on the engine—it just takes a lot longer. Rice, for example, can still be prepared, but it takes about six to eight hours. Eggs can be cooked, in hours rather than minutes.

The SatNav was still on the blink so we were again dependent on celestial sightings. I felt better after we rounded the outer reefs of Barbuda and could ease off onto a broad reach. We passed Barbuda in the middle of the night, glimpsing a few house lights on her shores. We could not relax until her low silhouette slipped off over the horizon.

We now settled into a routine at sea. We both went to sleep about three in the morning and slept in until about ten. I would get up and do some sun sights and Bob would get breakfast. I'd put the rice for dinner on the engine to cook and we'd start the engine to charge up the batteries and run the refrigeration. During the afternoon another round of sun sights would establish our position and we'd pull something out of the freezer to warm on the engine for dinner. The engine would be run another hour or so in the early evening, to charge the batteries again.

No SatNav, no propane, but at least the autopilot was still working. The fastpin we had finally succeeded in installing off the coast of Africa was still intact. One morning I awoke with a start. It was about nine local time and I had not heard anything. I simply had a premonition that I needed to get on deck fast. I rushed into the cockpit to see a large freighter sliding away to port about a quarter of a mile away. This was the main risk of short-handed sailing. We could not easily keep watches twenty-four hours a day, so we elected to sleep during the night hours. It was a risk, but generally a relatively low risk, because of the lack of shipping traffic. That, indeed, was the only vessel we saw until we approached the entrance to the Chesapeake.

About midnight on our fifth day at sea a force eight gale began to blow. Clouds had been building all day and it started to rain in the early evening. Seas rose up and by 10:00 P.M. were reaching ten feet. We continued to drive on. As midnight approached, I decided to shorten sail. I released the clew or metal loop on the aft corner of the main and tried to roll the sail into the mast, but the roller gear at the top of the mast jammed and she wouldn't roll. I tried to turn her one way, then the other. She still wouldn't work. I worked my way forward to the mast as the clew thrashed and slammed about. Suddenly it simply tore out of the tough sailcloth. I used a winch handle and one of the mast winches to release the tension on the mainsail halyard. She eased out of her groove and settled down onto the deck. The wind was now blowing about fifty knots and the seas were about twelve feet high. There was no moon out; it was pitch black. I struggled for about four hours trying to control the thrashing 460 square feet of sailcloth. Eventually, lying full length on the sail, I was able to draw portions of it underneath my body and lash it in sections to the deck. Bob kept asking if I was okay, but kept to our agreement not to leave the cockpit.

I then put up the storm trysail and dropped the genoa and we continued on under reduced canvas to slide away from the developing seas. Two days later we were becalmed, but gradually the wind worked its way around to forward of the beam at about eight knots. At this point, I needed not only our small 130 percent genoa, but a mainsail. Ours, however, was badly in need of repair, with the clew torn out and a large hole in the foot. I decided to try an experiment. I raised the drifter in the mainsail slot. Sheeting her tack directly to the deck, I brought the clew straight to a block on the stern, effectively excluding the boom. Bringing the sheet back to cockpit winch, we drew her out tightly and found that she was quite an effective rig. We sailed the next six hundred miles that way.

As we approached the Chesapeake, we started to see more ship traffic. I switched to Loran C navigation and we easily found the entrance to the bay. We rounded Cape Henry late in the afternoon of our tenth day at sea, soon tying up at a local dock in the tiny harbor at Little Creek, Virginia. The next morning we set off to work our way up the bay. We quickly learned one of the major lessons of sailing the waters of Chesapeake Bay. Everywhere there is thin water, and you need to be aware of the state of the tide before you go anywhere. I had studied the chart kit representation of Little Creek and it indicated plenty of water—twenty feet. Unfortunately, there was a place just off our dock where it shoaled to four feet, and there we settled in soft mud when we tried to leave. We had to wait three hours for the tide to rise enough to float us free. Finally, at noon, we again started to sail up the bay.

I had often contemplated the pleasures of sailing in Chesapeake Bay, but they eluded me this trip. The lower half of the bay is bereft of sheltering harbors and the northern half dealt us a powerful, driving storm with winds right on our nose, soaking rains, and temperatures in the low forties. We kept on under both engine and reefed sails, working our way first on one tack and then the other. It took us thirty-six hours of constant vigilance on the wheel, watching for marine traffic, avoiding shoals, and keeping track of lighthouses and other points of land for navigation before we reached our destination. Here, Bob truly showed his value on the trip. He kept watches off and on with me without complaint. We finally arrived in Oxford, Maryland, and slipped into a berth exhausted. That night I developed charley horses in the backs of both thighs that wracked me with pain. For the next week, I was so weak that I couldn't carry a suitcase for more than ten feet. Long sea voyages have a way of draining one's physical resources.

During the next year we found that the bottom had dropped out of the sailboat market. You couldn't give away good boats. I tried advertising, charter brokers, and even placed *Free Spirit* in a marina just outside the Annapolis Sailboat Show with a large pennant advertising her for sale. We got plenty of visitors, but no buyers. Even at sixty percent of her original cost, we could not develop a buyer. Finally, we decided to sail her back to Boston to try and find a buyer there.

Young John, then thirteen years old, joined me for this trip. We sailed up to the head of the bay, motored through the Chesapeake and Delaware Canal and down through Delaware Bay. At Cape May we were joined by a couple of very good friends, Dave and B. K. We had a very pleasant and uneventful sail up to Newport. After three enjoyable days there, John and I took her on a thrilling sleighride down the full length of Buzzard's Bay. We drove under twenty-five knots of following winds and easy three-foot seas to turn in for the evening in Onset. The next day we sailed into Boston Harbor, completing our circumnavigation of the Atlantic after a bit over three years' time.

Closing the Circle

Our friends at Constitution Marina welcomed us back and found space for us to tie up, and there we spun sea stories well into the evening.

The following year we chartered *Free Spirit* to ease the financial burden and, after three years, we paid off our debts. *Free Spirit* was taken off the used boat market and I have continued to upgrade her condition. Now we are beginning to look forward to new adventures at sea. Plans include a Bermuda race in 1989 and further trips to the Caribbean in future years. The joys and rigors of sailing have seeped into the family's pores. We now think of our little ship and of the sea as integral parts of our existence.

Afterword

*E*vents in twentieth-century America pressure families in ways never experienced in earlier times. Previous generations lived together, worked together, and developed close and lasting ties that made the word *family* have a kinship with self. Modern transportation, the primacy of income and career over intimacy and personal relations, and the materialistic values espoused in all too many aspects of our culture have devalued the permanence of home and hearth.

One casualty of this societal neurosis has been relations between teenagers and parents. Parents are out working (indeed, the majority of families have two working parents) while the children are brought up by the schools and their peers. The parents are the overseers, but are responsible in absentia. The resulting disaffection between teens and their parents is of epidemic proportions.

As I see it, the close proximity to each other and the need to work together for mutual safety on our trip across the Atlantic created bonds of friendship and mutual esteem within our family. I, for one, could more clearly see the capabilities of my children as a result of the voyage.

Their obvious desire to help me deal with the crises and problems of life at sea taught me to respect them in new ways. Subtly, they became more than just my children. They were my crew, an intimate part of the functioning of our ship and our adventure. When they left us in Bergen to return to school, the entire atmosphere of the ship changed. No longer did we have youthful ebullience to spice up our days. Although Cindy and I still had no difficulty meeting people on the remainder of our cruise, we began to realize how special it was to have our children along to break the ice in port after port.

Recently, when I presented the prospect of sailing in the 1989 Marion/Bermuda race to my children, each of them leapt at the chance to be a part of the crew. In fact, two of them are going. John has chosen to be skipper this time. His older brother will be a watch captain, and I will be the navigator.

John has enthusiastically begun the work needed to refine his skills so that he can assume the captain's responsibilities. He is picking his own crew, defining their roles, learning the details of chart-reading and trip-planning, and will, over the next several months, find out just how much is involved in planning an ocean voyage.

The hope was that the transatlantic adventure would cement our family's relationships with each other. It succeeded beyond my wildest dreams.

How to Prepare for an Ocean Voyage

*P*reparation for an ocean voyage is a demanding science that requires careful thought and planning. The intention here is to offer a guide to such preparation, and to clarify the pitfalls and dangers that should be of concern. A long-distance ocean voyage is as different from coastal sailing as a trip to outer space is from a flight to a nearby city. It is more like scaling Mount Everest than taking a hike into town.

The ocean is unpredictable. It's possible to sail to Bermuda in light to moderate winds with clear blue skies and fluffy, fair-weather clouds. With a week of light weather conditions prior to sailing, the seas might well be down. There may be no distant storms to send endless reaches of twelve-foot rollers to mar the serenity of the voyage. My experience, however, and that of countless other sailors, is that the sea is often harsh and cold, weather conditions are changeable and can be frighteningly violent, and the longer you are at sea, the greater your chances of getting clobbered.

In considering the type of boat for an ocean trip one

should look for stability. A shallow draft, beamy vessel with a high center of gravity will, if turned turtle, stay there. It may be *more* stable in the upside down position with its mast in the water than it is right side up. Don't go to sea in such a boat. You want solid, stiff construction. Whether a boat is of light, medium, or heavy displacement, quality of construction and stiffness of the hull and deck are of vital concern. Have the boat surveyed and describe your plans for her to the surveyor. He will be able to advise you on how to prepare her for sea so your risks are minimized.

What is your boat like in moderate conditions with winds blowing twenty to thirty knots? Does she sail on her ear? You will be very uncomfortable spending a week or more at a forty-degree angle of heel. Much better to find a boat that is stiff enough in those conditions to sail at twenty degrees. What is her displacement? Light displacement boats will usually have faster passages, but will have an increased risk of hull damage in extreme conditions or upon colliding with a solid object at sea (barrel, container, log, boat, rock, or whale). The spars on a light displacement boat have a greater incidence of failure, as they are usually designed to cut windage and weight. A fast passage may mean five days at sea rather than eight, but a lot can happen in five days on the ocean.

Anything that can prevent the need to go on deck in a blow is of value. Roller-furling sails of all types should be considered for the main as well as the foresails. A running forestay can be kept at the shrouds when not in use and set on a quick release lever. This will allow you to set a working or storm jib without having to drop the big roller-furling genoa. Alternately, a staysail stay can permit you to run up working or storm sails and may even be set on roller-furling.

A storm trysail of adequate size, perhaps twenty to twenty-five percent of the size of your mainsail should be permanently set in a bag at the foot of the mast, with its slides in their own sail track to one side of the main track. This allows a quick hoist in rough conditions and will let you douse the main and tie down a wildly swinging boom while you sheet the storm trysail to a heavy block on your stern.

This points up a little-known fact. Many boats do not heave to well under the traditional backed jib and trimmed, reefed mainsail. They will actually fall off the wind and lie beam on to the seas. These same boats will lie nicely, head up to the wind, with a storm trysail or triple-reefed main sheeted in tightly and the helm brought over hard to weather. The trysail isn't big enough to drive the bow through the eye of the wind but holds the head up to the gale nicely. If you think your boat won't heave to, try this little trick. Even with a boat that will heave to with a backed storm jib, just using the trysail is a safer and more reliable way of handling storm conditions and can be carried in worse weather. Backing your jib and sheeting in the main is okay in a smoky southwester in Buzzard's Bay when you want to stop for lunch, but not for a storm at sea.

Finally, you do not want a massive cockpit that can be easily swamped. This will drag the stern down and prevent her from lifting to the seas. The cockpit should be self-bailing and the drains should be large enough to drain her in two or three minutes. You must be able to secure cockpit lockers, and they should have adequate rubber gaskets to prevent the ingress of water at extreme angles of heel. A raised bridge deck to protect the cabin from a flooded cockpit, and sturdy companionway slides that can be fixed in place with a throughbolt, shock cord, or other such means, should be considered.

Personal safety equipment should include safety harnesses with extra strong metal fasteners and webbing for each member of the crew. Have them aboard and please, please use them! Personal strobes and man-overboard poles and drills are all well and good, but are meant to correct a serious mistake. The best treatment is prevention. Such mistakes must never happen. It is extremely difficult to maneuver a vessel in rough conditions and pluck someone from the water. Jacklines should be strung from the rear stay to the mast and from the mast to the bow. All crew should clip on before they leave the safety of the cabin and should stay attached until they go below again. Having the jacklines in the center of the boat allows crew to reach the line from the safety of the companionway ladder and eliminates the need to unclip from one line and reattach to another simply to move from one side of the cockpit to the other. The slight inconvenience of having to use a harness is far outweighed by the security of knowing that you or your crew will not disappear at sea. You may also want to consider double lifelines with stanchions through-bolted to the hull, and a safety net if there will be children aboard. Do not allow your crew to go to the rail except in absolutely calm conditions. Many a body has been recovered at sea with his fly undone. In bad weather and at night, when a trip to the head is not easily accomplished, have the crew use a plastic bottle with a secure cap. Later dump that overboard or into the cockpit drains if everything is wet anyway. Have women use a plastic bedpan, obtainable from many pharmacies. Privacy can be assured with a modicum of consideration for your crew's feelings.

As for the boat's interior, one should strive to prevent the crew below from being struck by flying objects, or themselves becoming airborne. To ensure this, each crew should have his own lee cloth at least sixty inches wide attached to his bunk. Nylon netting is often more comfortable than stiffer cloth and may be cooler. When clipped to the cabin wall above the berth, a lee cloth will hold one in like a cocoon. All drawers should be positively secured, either with ties or latches, so the contents don't fly about the boat in a knockdown. You'll want adequate handholds, and rounded corners on all furniture help prevent bruises or more serious injury. You may want to consider a gimballed stove. Radios, sextants, books, refrigerator tops, and kettles on the stove can all be potentially lethal, so find a secure place for everything and secure everything in its place.

Batteries should be in permanently positioned boxes with tops that are secured so they can't come out even if you turn turtle. Ventilators should have screw-on covers for the ultimate storm. Anchors *must* be tied down or they won't stay on your bowsprit. Pumps must all be in working order. I would recommend that every seagoing boat invest in three types of pumps: one or preferably two manual high-output bilge pumps, an electric bilge pump with a strainer, and an emergency, engine-driven, very high-output pump such as that produced by Jabsco for potential disasters. A bilge-water alarm and a gas detector are also useful. If you plan to go to high latitudes, consider a diesel furnace.

Other valuable items that you may want aboard your vessel can run the gamut from a life raft, man-overboard poles, emergency supply canister, a masthead tricolor light, radar reflector, and assorted communications equipment such as single side band or ham radio, VHF radio, emergency position indicating radio beacon (EPIRB). Coast Guard-required safety equipment includes life preservers, flares, horn, bell, and fire extinguishers. Various sizes of tapered wooden plugs, underwater epoxy, spare parts, and tools should also be carried. Radar is a luxury, but in fog can become a necessity. It's either that or worry a lot. The newest units are modest in cost, within the reach of many sailors today. Radar is also a great boon to local piloting and navigation. Radomes (radar emitting beacons visible on the boat's radar) in the tide-ripped waters between the Isle of Wight and the Brittany coast of France kept us on course in heavy fog when little else would.

All ports and hatches should be inspected for strength and security before you put to sea. If you have any doubts, build storm shutters out of Lexan and use them. Make sure that you have access to the stuffing gland of your propeller shaft so that it can be tightened if it develops a leak. Put a hose clamp both on your propeller shaft and on the rudder post; if either decides to part company with the boat, the clamp won't allow them to fit out the through-hull and will prevent a disastrous flood.

At least three anchors should be carried. Five would not be too many. Two CQRs and a yachtsman or Herreshoff anchor are of the most value. One of your anchors should have 200 feet of chain and a windlass to work it. The other may be equipped with 12 feet of chain and 250 feet of line. The CQR holds well in sand and mud and has more holding power than the Danforth in borderline conditions. The yachtsman will hold on coral, rock, or kelp. I have designed a fitting for the bow pulpit that permits this anchor to be kept on deck ready for use at all times. The Bruce anchor holds well in mud and sand but does not dig in well in hard-packed sand or kelp. I do not recommend it, as it has no advantages over the CQR and does have several limitations. The Danforth is a nice, easily stowed, all-round anchor for coastal sailing and lunch hooks in New England waters. It might be carried for your fourth anchor, but is useless in the Caribbean and many other areas.

Check all your seacocks for ease of use and lack of corrosion. Have double hose clamps on all hoses leading to the seacocks. Ground your mast to the keel with #0–#2 cable as a protection against lightning damage. Get all the charts you will need for both the crossing and any ports you might need to visit on the way in case of an emergency.

For long-distance voyagers, a SatNav is a valuable, modestly priced piece of equipment and has great accuracy. For the long-distance voyager who leaves the safety net of coastal United States' Loran C chains, there is no better method of fixing your position. Best of all, SatNav is there every day and night, often several times a day, with an updated position in any kind of weather. While you certainly should bring your sextant and know how to use it, because any electrical device can break down, don't scorn the benefits of today's technology. Too many good navigators have been fooled by currents or have been prevented by cloudy skies from taking celestial observations. The bones of their vessels litter the seas. The technology is available. Take advantage of it.

Some form of self-steering is vital for the lightly crewed yacht at sea. It is too cold in the North Atlantic to stand interminable watches in forty degree weather with cold rain and twenty-five knots of wind slowly but inexorably freezing each molecule in your feet and working up from there. Do that six hours a day for three weeks and see how you feel about ocean sailing! Either an autopilot or a windvane is valuable. Each has its advantages and disadvantages. The windvane requires no power to run and works well for the small vessel with limited power and fuel capacity. It is useless, however, when you must power your way through calms, canals, or fjords. It frequently does not work well in light airs or on downwind reaches unless half a gale is blowing. To my mind, if you have the fuel capacity to run your engine to charge the batteries for three to four hours daily for the length of your cruise, then a good autopilot has it all over the windvane. It can be used in virtually all conditions under sail or power and is worth its weight in gold.

Good foul-weather gear should be tested at home first, before going to sea. Do not stint on quality here. If you don't have dry pants, you will become chilled and suffer from hypothermia. This can seriously impair your ability to function. Immerse the seat of the pants in cold water in your bathtub. Does the inside stay dry? If not, return them and get a different brand.

A medical kit should cover all the usual illnesses that are possible and for which expert help is not available. At least cover the basics: sea sickness, headaches, diarrhea, constipation, urinary infections, vaginitis, respiratory infections, staph infections, allergies, cuts, eye injuries, and broken bones. Appendix C lists recommended items for a medical kit.

Finally, I know that in spite of all the precautions listed above, the outrageous expense involved, and the hazards and discomforts attendant on heading to sea, many reading these pages will do so some day. Read some of the excellent books on the subject. If you are a romantic who strives for new challenges, go out and slay your dragon; but take the time and care to ensure that there are no chinks in your armor.

A QUICK CHECKLIST FOR OFFSHORE SAFETY

- Formal survey of your vessel
- Three anchors with chain and rode
- Tiedowns for the anchors/chain stopper
- Double lifelines/netting forward
- Secure stanchions/backing plates
- Large cockpit drains
- Jacklines in centerline of boat
- Storm trysail on separate track
- Reliable furling systems for sails
- Locker security clasps and gaskets
- Tiedown for companionway slides
- Ventilator caps
- Radar reflector
- Autopilot/windvane
- Canistered life raft/emergency supplies
- Man-overboard pole(s) and horseshoes
- Tiedowns or latches for drawers, refrigerator top, floorboards, books, pots, any loose items
- Lee cloths for *each* crew member
- Safety harnesses for *each* crew member
- EPIRB (Emergency Position Indicating Radio Beacon)
- Tapered plugs and underwater epoxy
- Pumps (electric, engine driven, manual)
- Check seacocks for function and deterioration
- Gas detector/bilge-water alarm
- Separate water supplies (at least two tanks/separate shutoffs)
- Medications: See Appendix C

Your Offshore Sailing Medical Kit

*T*his is merely a list and descriptions of medications that I believe may be useful for the offshore sailing vessel. These are *not* prescriptions or recommendations for use. The reader should be clearly aware that the brief explanations given do not adequately differentiate between various antibiotics and their specific uses, nor is it possible in this brief space to discuss thoroughly the problems attendant on the diagnosis and treatment of illness. For further information, I recommend that you read one of the excellent books now available on the subject. My own book, *The Boater's Medical Companion*, is scheduled for publication by Cornell Maritime Press in the fall of 1989.

> 2-inch Ace bandages
> 70% alcohol (to neutralize jelly fish stings)
> alcohol swabs
> Band-aids
> Betadine swabs (antiseptic for cleaning wounds)
> butterfly bandages
> cotton balls

eye patches
4 × 4-inch sterile gauze pads
2-inch gauze roller bandage
2-inch nylon tape
oral thermometer
3-inch wide strip vaseline gauze

Actifed
aloe sunburn cream or lotion
Ampicillin 500 mg (antibiotic; for prescription and use, consult your doctor)
antacids: Gelusil tablets or Maalox
aspirin
Benadryl 25 mg (antihistamine for allergic reactions)
codeine sulfate 30 mg (prescribed for pain)
Colace 100 mg (for constipation)
Compazine suppositories 5 mg (for seasickness, nausea; by prescription)
chewable vitamin C 500 mg
Dicloxacillin 250 mg
erythromycin 500 mg (family of systemic antibiotics for infection; consult your doctor for specific prescription and indications for use)
0.5% hydrocortisone cream (for minor skin irritations)
hydrogen peroxide (helps dissolve wax impacted in ears)
Immodium (for diarrhea)
Keflex 500 mg (an antibiotic; consult your physician for prescription and appropriate use)
Metamucil (very effective for constipation, yet mild)
Monistat vaginal tablets (prescribed for vaginitis)
Motrin 400 mg (prescription useful for premenstrual cramps) (Advil is a nonprescription substitute)
Neosporin eye ointment (topical antibiotic, by prescription)

Neosporin, polymyxin-B, hydrocortisone ear drops (prescription for external ear infections)

Phenergan expectorant with codeine (effective cough syrup, by prescription)

prednisone 10 mg (antiinflammatory agent; see your doctor for directions and prescription for specific brand)

1% silver sulfidiazine cream (antibiotic cream prescribed for severe burns)

Slo-Phyllin 250 mg (bronchodilator prescribed for asthma) Primatene tablets are a weak, but effective substitute

Stugeron (Cinnarizine 15 mg, available only in Europe, Canada, and Bermuda; the most effective seasickness remedy)

sunburn lotions (#8, #15, and #20 sunburn protection; get PABA-free lotion if anyone is allergic to PABA)

Tagamet 300 mg (eliminates acid in the stomach; prescribed for ulcer patients)

tetracycline 250 mg (antibiotic; your physician can prescribe a specific brand and advise you as to use)

Tylenol extra strength

vinegar (to neutralize the poison from sea urchin punctures)

zinc oxide cream (soothing for skin irritations)

Glossary of Nautical Terms

Abaft—Behind, to the rear.

Aft—The rear portion of the boat.

Anchor locker—A closed compartment with an entry door, which holds the anchor chain for the main anchor on one side and an anchor rode for the smaller secondary anchor on the other. A partition divides the two sides.

Autopilot—A mechanical device powered by the ship's batteries, using an internal compass that can control the direction of the ship. It uses a motor-driven chain to turn the rudder.

Backstay—A heavy stainless steel wire that is attached to the back of the mast near the masthead. It supports the mast and adjusts the degree of mast rake (the amount that the mast is angled forward or backward from true vertical).

Beam—The width of the boat at its widest point.

Beam reach—Sailing in such a direction that the wind comes directly over the side or beam of the boat.

Beat—The closest one can sail into the wind without stopping completely (going into irons).

Berth—A bunk or bed aboard ship; also, the place where a yacht ties up at a dock.

Bilge—The space under the cabin sole (floor) used for storage and, in deeper parts of the boat, allows for the accumulation of modest amounts of water so that the rest of the interior of the boat will not be soaked.

Binnacle—A post that supports the wheel, compass, and wind speed/depth instruments.

Block—The nautical term for a pulley.

Boom—A long rigid spar, or heavy pole. The bottom end of the mainsail is attached to the boom.

Bow—The forward end of the boat.

Bow pulpit—A stainless steel rail sweeping around the bow at waist height; it is designed to prevent someone from going overboard when working in the bow.

Bowsprit—A heavily constructed stainless steel plate protruding over the bow that contains a pair of rollers. It is used to guide anchor chain in and out of the boat.

Brigantine—An older design of sailing ship with two masts. The forward mast is square-rigged, while the main mast uses a fore and aft sail. The topsail is also a square sail.

Broad reach—Sailing with the wind "abaft the beam," that is, with the wind coming from back of the beam.

Bulkhead—A bearing wall within the boat that helps support the deck and acts as a room divider.

Catboat—A sailboat with one mast set right at the bow of the boat. It has a mainsail but no jib.

CCA—Cruising Club of America.

CCA Rule—The accepted racing rule used during major ocean races during the 1950s. Boats designed to this rule had long overhangs fore and aft, short waterlines for their overall length, and relatively narrow beam.

Chain gypsy—Grooved circular metal plate that grips the chain hauled by an anchor windlass.

Chainplate—A heavy stainless steel plate embedded into the fiberglass of the deck of a boat and bolted into supporting frames within the boat. It is used to support the mast of the boat by acting as a fixed point to which side shrouds and fore and aft stays can be securely attached.

Chain stripper—A metal bar that prevents anchor chain from jamming in the chain gypsy. When the chain strikes the bar, it is forced away from the gypsy into a chain locker.

Chart—A marine map.

Chock—A heavy fitting of stainless steel, placed on the rail; it guides a docking line and prevents damage to the rail.

Cleat—A heavy metal fitting to which you attach lines.

Clevis pin—A heavy-duty stainless steel pin used to pin a turnbuckle into position on a chainplate.

Clew—The aft corner of a sail.

Close reach—Sailing with the wind coming from a direction ahead of the beam of the boat.

Coach roof—The roof of a boat's cabin.

Coaming—The backs of the seats in the cockpit.

Cockpit—Open area in the rear of the boat containing seats, steering wheel, and engine and autopilot controls. In "center cockpit" designs, it is placed farther forward.

Cockpit lockers—Roomy lockers below the seats in the cockpit. They hold spare sails, lines, fenders, and gear.

Companionway—Entrance from the cockpit to the interior of the cabin, sometimes containing a ladder.

Compass—A device used to determine direction via a magnetic needle set on a card that floats in a fluid.

Compass rose—A representation on a chart of the positions of the compass. Both magnetic compass direction and true positions of north, south, east, and west are indicated.

Cowl vents—Hooded ventilators with an elevated pipe within them. They allow ventilation belowdecks without permitting water to enter.

CQR—Type of anchor, also called a plow anchor, of heavy construction and with a plow shape designed to dig into mud or sand.

Cutter—A sailboat with one mast and two stays (supporting wires) forward of the mast. The head stay runs from the top of the mast to the bow. The second stay extends from a distance three-quarters of the way up the mast to a spot several feet aft of where the headstay is attached to the bow. Headsails can be attached to both of these stays. The forward one supports the jib and the one farther aft supports a staysail.

Cyclone—An atmospheric disturbance characterized by a circular flow of air around a low-pressure system. In its extreme forms, it is another name for a hurricane, and has wind strengths in excess of sixty-four knots or seventy-five miles per hour.

Danforth—A lightweight (given its holding power) anchor with twin pointed flukes that dig into sand and heavy mud.

Dead reckoning—The art of estimating one's position by determining the course one has sailed and estimating the speed at which one has been sailing.

Deck—The exterior top of the boat.

Depth-sounder—An electronic device that sends sound waves to the bottom of the body of water and records the time it takes for these to bounce back to a detector on board.

Deviation—The number of degrees by which the compass is inaccurate due to magnetic interference on the boat.

Dinghy—A small boat used to ferry people and supplies from boat to shore.

Dividers—A two-pronged device used to measure distances on a chart.

Docking line—A strong nylon line having the ability to stretch under load. It is used to tie the boat up to a dock. At least two and often three lines are used: a bow line, holding the bow to a cleat on the dock forward of the bow; a stern line, holding the stern of the boat to a place on the dock aft of the boat; and a spring line, used to hold the center of the boat to a place either forward or aft to prevent movement of the boat in an undesirable direction.

Downwind—A position farther from the source of the wind than another object.

Draft—The lowest point of the boat under water.

Fastpin—A strong stainless steel pin with a compressible knob at one end and a stainless ring at the other. It can be quickly placed in a hole and will not slip out, as it is held in place by the knob and the ring. It is usually used to prevent a metal bar from moving, or sail slides from coming out of their groove when a sail is dropped.

Fender—A rubber, air-filled cylinder tied to the exterior of the boat to prevent the topsides from being damaged by another boat or a dock.

Fin keel—A short, deep keel having the appearance of a fin.

Fix—An accurate position determined by comparing two or more lines of position.

Flog—The flapping of a sail in the wind when it is out of control.

Fluke—A pointed tip on the end of an anchor that allows it to dig into the ocean bottom.

Foot—The bottom edge of a sail; also, the bottom of the mast.

Force—A method of measuring wind strengths. Force seven

is a wind strength of twenty-eight to thirty-three knots or thirty-two to thirty-eight miles per hour, a moderate gale. Force eight is a wind strength of thirty-four to forty knots or thirty-nine to forty-six miles per hour, or a fresh gale. Force nine is a wind strength of forty-one to forty-seven knots or forty-seven to fifty-four miles per hour, and is called a strong gale. Force ten is a wind strength of forty-eight to fifty-five knots or forty-five to sixty-three miles per hour, and is called a whole gale. Force twelve is a wind strength of sixty-four to seventy-one knots or seventy-three to eighty-two miles per hour, and is the beginning of the forces of hurricane winds. (From Stuart Walker's book, *Wind and Strategy*.)

Forepeak—The narrow section of the interior of the boat well forward in the bow.

Furl—To fold or roll up a sail in preparation for putting it away.

Gale—Wind forces in excess of about thirty miles per hour and less than hurricane force. (See "Force" above.)

Gelcoat—A thin, relatively impervious layer used to cover the exterior of the fiberglass of the boat to give it a painted appearance.

Genoa—A foresail or headsail that extends behind the mast.

Genny—Another term for genoa.

Gimballed—Placed on pintles allowing the item to remain relatively horizontal with the surface of the water despite the angle of heel of the boat. Most stoves on cruising boats are gimballed.

Halyard—A line used to haul a sail up the mast.

Hand—To lower a sail.

Hanging locker—A closet in the cabin in which clothes can be hung.

Harness—A strongly constructed garment made of webbing that is used to hold a crew member to part of the boat. Worn over the upper half of the body for safety at night or during stormy weather.

Hatch—A door that closes off an opening to the deck.

Head—Marine toilet; also, the top of something such as the mast.

Head board—A metal board sewn into the top corner of the mainsail for strength.

Head stay—The wire that supports the forward part of the mast and extends from the top of the mast to the bow of the boat. It also supports the head sail (storm jib, jib, genoa).

Heave to—To position the boat so that it lies slightly off the wind and stays in position, gently drifting slowly away from the wind, or leeward.

Heel—To lean. A boat will heel over when the wind strikes the sails from the side, exerting a force that tips the boat away from the wind.

Herreshoff—A heavy-duty anchor constructed with two large curving flukes at 180° to each other, a heavy stock, and two bars at right angles to the flukes. Very useful for anchoring in difficult conditions, such as rock. Named after the famous turn-of-the-century yacht designer, builder, and master sailor, Nathaniel Herreshoff. The anchors are currently made by Paul Luke in Boothbay Harbor, Maine.

H.O. 249—A book of tables for calculating the position of the sun. It is designed for airplane navigation, but is commonly used by small-boat navigators.

Hull—The body of the boat.

Hurricane—A cyclonic storm with wind strengths in excess of 64 knots. Winds in excess of 175 knots or 200 miles per hour have been recorded.

Irons—The position a boat takes when it is facing directly into the wind. The sails are flogging and the boat will only drift backward.

Jacklines—Lines strung the length of the boat from bow to stern on either side. They serve as a place to fasten the crew's safety harness, and as a handhold to help prevent crew from going overboard. They are among the most important safety devices used by offshore sailors.

Jib—A sail set on the head stay. It is never larger than the foretriangle of the boat, that is, it does not extend behind the mast (see "genoa").

Jibe—Turning the boat so that the wind comes from one side of the stern to the other. This will cause the mainsail to swing over to the opposite side of the boat. A jibe is simply a downwind tack.

Kedge—When grounded, to haul one's vessel clear by setting an anchor some distance from the boat and hauling the boat over to the anchor; also, as noun, a plow anchor.

Keel—The vertical, fixed appendage below the waterline whose function is to prevent leeway or sideslipping.

Ketch—A two-masted sailing vessel whose rear mast (mizzen) is shorter than its forward or main mast. The rear mast is set *forward* of the rudder post (see "yawl").

Knot—A nautical mile (6,000 feet).

Lay—To be able to follow a course or direction; also, the arrangement of the strands of a rope.

Lee—The side of a boat away from the wind; also, the protected side of an island or other land mass.

Leeway—Unintentional sideslipping of a sailing boat as it moves forward.

Lifelines—Plastic-covered wire strung at least eighteen inches off the deck on stainless poles (stanchions) at the edge of the deck from bow pulpit to stern pulpit. They are intended to help prevent crew from going overboard.

Life raft—An inflatable rubber raft with a canopy, which can be quickly launched in an emergency.

Line—A rope on a boat that is not used for anchoring (rode), hauling up sails (halyard), or hauling out the clew of a sail (sheets). Ropes on a boat are given specific names so that they are not confused when a skipper is giving an order. If the skipper orders you to release the main halyard, there should be no question in your mind which line he is referring to.

Locker—Any enclosed space on a boat used for storage.

Log—The ship's record of progress and conditions at sea; also, a recording device designed to measure the distance sailed.

Loran—Long-distance radio aid to navigation. This device is a combination of radio receiver and computer, which times the receipt of various radio signals and compares them with a master signal. The time difference received gives a fairly accurate estimate of one's geographical position.

Mainsail—The sail attached to the mast (or to the taller mast in the case of a ketch or yawl). Also known simply as the "main."

Mainsheet—The line that holds the boom down and adjusts the position of the boom and thereby the mainsail.

Mast head—The top of the mast.

Mizzen—The second or shorter mast on a ketch or a yawl; also, the sail placed on that mast.

Mooring—A permanent heavy object (e.g., a mushroom anchor) placed on the bottom and attached by a chain to a float on the surface, to which a boat is tied in an anchorage.

Nautical mile—A knot, 6,000 feet (slightly more than the 5,280 feet in a statute or land mile).

Nav. station—Area of boat devoted to navigation: consists of a table and bench with nearby electronic and radio devices.

Nose—The bow or in the direction of the bow.

Overhang—The amount that the bow or stern at the level of the deck overhangs the same portion of the boat at the waterline.

Pad eye—A U-shaped fitting fixed to the deck or a spar, containing an opening through which a line can pass. It helps to hold the line in that position.

Parallel rules—Instrument used to transfer a line to another parallel position on a chart.

Perch—A wooden pole set in the bottom of a waterway, rising above the surface, marked with an arrow indicating the preferred channel.

Plow—Wedge-shaped anchor of heavy construction (see also "CQR").

Port—The left-hand side of the boat (as seen when facing forward).

Practique—Permission given by a foreign customs agent to enter a country.

Preventer—A line placed on the boom and led forward. It's purpose is to prevent the boom from accidentally swinging over to the other side (see "jibe").

Quarantine flag—A yellow "Q" flag that is raised at the spreader to indicate that your boat has just arrived in a foreign country and requests customs clearance.

Quarter—A direction represented by an imaginary line running out at a forty-five-degree angle from either corner of the stern.

Radar—High-frequency radio waves emitted by a radar

antenna (or magnetron), which bounce off objects such as other boats and can be detected and represented on a screen by an onboard receiver. It is used to locate hazards at sea when visibility is poor.

Radar reflector—A metallic, multifaceted object that reflects radar and can thereby be easily seen with a radar unit. A radar reflector increases the likelihood that one's vessel will be seen by other ships at sea.

Rail—The outer edge of the boat.

Rake—The angle applied to the mast to pull it aft or forward of standing straight up. Affects the shape of a mainsail.

Reef—To shorten or otherwise decrease the area of a sail.

Relay—An electronic device that responds to a current change by activating a switch to send current through the device.

Rode—A line used to attach an anchor to the boat.

Roller-furling—A device used to roll up a sail in its working position.

Rudder—A movable vertical device placed toward the stern of the boat below the surface of the water. It is used to help the boat change directions.

Run—The direction a boat takes when the wind is coming from directly over the stern.

Running lights—Three lights required of all boats, to be used under conditions of reduced visibility: a red light carried to port and covering an arc of 45° from directly forward to directly abeam of the ship; a green light carried to starboard just opposite the red light. And a 135° white light carried on the stern.

SatNav—A computerized radio receiver that picks up communications from sattelites in orbit. These assist the boat in periodically getting accurate navigational fixes.

Schooner—A two-masted sailboat; the two masts are almost the same height.

Seacock—A shutoff valve through which a hose can exit the bottom of the boat.

Self-bailing—The ability of a boat to bail itself automatically. Usually a feature in the cockpit of cruising boats to empty out the cockpit when it is filled by boarding waves.

Sextant—A device used to measure the angle of the sun or other heavenly body from the horizon.

Sheet—A line attached to the clew of a sail.

Shift lever—The lever that lets the engine change gears from forward to neutral and to reverse.

Shroud—A heavy wire connecting the top of the mast to the side of the boat.

Single side band—An AM radio band with greater range than VHF radio.

Skeg—A vertical, fixed appendage, smaller than the keel, placed aft just in front of the rudder. It makes it easier to steer the boat.

Skerry—A tiny, rocky islet.

Sloop—A single-masted boat with only two sails up at any one time.

Snatch block—A pulley that can be quickly unclipped and moved to another position.

Sole—The floor of the cabin.

Spar—A major supporting device for the sails, that is, a mast or boom.

Spinnaker—A large, free-standing sail carried forward of the mast and fixed at the head to the mast, at the tack to a pole, and to the clew by a sheet. It is used for downwind work.

Spreader—A horizontal pole attached on either side of the mast at least halfway up toward the top and used to hold the shrouds out away from the mast to increase the efficiency of their pull on the masthead.

Spring line—A line attached to the middle of the boat leading to a place on the dock well forward or aft of that position. It is used to keep the boat from drifting too far away from the dock and from moving forward or aft in any significant way.

Starboard—The right-hand side of the boat as seen when facing forward on deck.

Stay—A wire support for the mast, either forward or aft.

Staysail—A small sail set aft of the head stay on a small or baby stay.

Stem fitting—The forward fitting on the boat to which the head stay is attached.

Stern—The aft or rear of the boat.

Storm—A low-pressure system in which the wind strengths are of gale force or higher.

Storm jib—A small, heavily constructed sail intended to be used on the head stay in storm conditions.

Storm trysail—a small, heavily constructed sail intended to be used in place of the mainsail in storm conditions.

Strobe—A high-intensity flashing light.

Tack—To change direction in such a way that the boom moves from one side of the boat to the other. During this maneuver, the bow of the boat moves through the eye of the wind.

Tender—Quickly and easily heeled, referring to a boat that will lean to a relatively gentle breeze; also, as noun, a dinghy.

Throttle—Lever used to increase the acceleration of the engine.

Through-hull—Opening in the hull for the intake or elimination of fluids. Attached via a seacock to a hose.

Topping lift—A wire attached from the masthead to the

end of the boom. Used to prevent the boom from falling onto the deck when the mainsail is furled.

Topsides—The sides of the exterior of the hull above the waterline; also, above the deck as opposed to in the cabin.

Transom—The back of the stern of the boat.

Trysail—A small triangular sail used in place of the mainsail in heavy wind conditions.

Turnbuckle—A device used to adjust the tension of stays and shrouds.

Twin running sails or twins—Matched large jibs attached to each other by a common luff wire, used for downwind work in place of a spinnaker.

Vang—A line to hold down the boom and keep it horizontal when the wind is abaft the beam.

Variation—The deflection of a compass needle away from true north due to the geographical separation of magnetic north from the North Pole (geographic north).

VHF radio—Very high frequency radio, used for short-range communication (up to fifty miles).

Waterline—The place on the hull where the surface of the water meets the hull.

Wheel—The steering wheel.

Whisker pole—A sturdy spar used to hold out a genoa for downwind reaching.

Windlass—A powerful winch used to raise the heavy anchor.

Yankee—A high-clewed genoa.

Yawl—A two-masted sailboat with the small aft mast placed behind the rudder post.

Asbjørnsen, Peter Christen, *Norwegian Fairy Tales*. Translated by Helen and John Gade. New York: The American–Scandinavian Foundation, 1924.

Bergmann, Leola Nelson, *Americans from Norway*. Philadelphia and New York: J. B. Lippincott Co., 1950.

Blegen, Theodore C., *Land of Their Choice*. Minneapolis: University of Minnesota Press, 1955.

Buckley, Christopher, "Norway, The Commandos' Dieppe." Her Majesty's Stationery Office, 1952.

Gattiome-Hordy, G. M., "Norway and the War." Oxford Pamphlets of World Affairs, 1941.

Logan, F. Donald, *The Vikings in History*. Totowa, N.J.: Barnes & Noble, 1983.

Magnusson, Magnus, *Vikings*. New York: E. P. Dutton, 1980.

Martineau, Harriet, *Norway and the Norwegians*. Tales for the people and their children or feats on the fjord. (Published in the 19th century; can be found in the rare books section of the Wellesley College Library.)

Qualey, Carlton C., *Norwegian Settlement in the United States*. Norwegian American Historical Association, 1938.

Worm-Miller, Jacob, *Norway Revolts against the Nazis*. Lindsay Drummond, Great Britain, 1941.